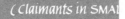
(Claimants in SMA...

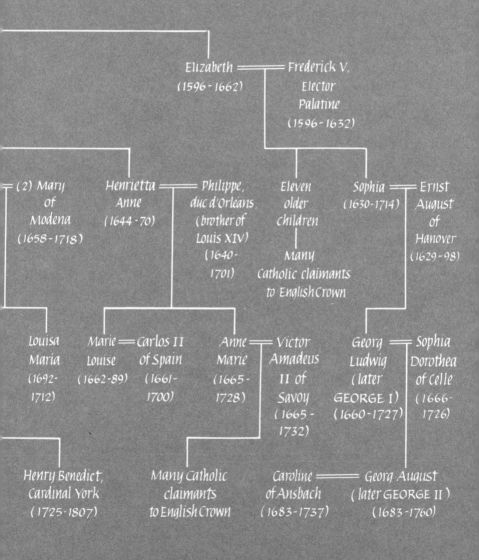

FALSE DAWN

FALSE DAWN

FALSE DAWN

Women in the
Age of the Sun King

Louis Auchincloss

ANCHOR PRESS
Doubleday & Company, Inc.
GARDEN CITY, NEW YORK
1984

Library of Congress Cataloging in Publication Data
Auchincloss, Louis.
  False dawn.
  Bibliography: p.
  Includes index.
  1. Women—Europe—History—17th century.
  2. Women—Europe—Biography.   I. Title.
  HQ1148.A85   1984   305.4'094
  ISBN 0-385-18021-7
Library of Congress Catalog Card Number 82–45620

To my learned friend and former associate in law
Henry N. Ess, III
Invaluable guide in reading history

Contents

I

Women and
the Sun King

The women we shall discover in these pages were English, Italian, German and Swedish, as well as French, but all of them, like most European men and women of the era, are seen in some relation to the far-spreading rays of the Sun King. Louis XIV, for better or worse (and there was quite as much worse as better), dominated Europe throughout a reign that lasted from his accession in 1643 at the age of four to his death seventy-two years later. His development of huge standing armies, by means of which he pushed his frontiers into the Spanish Netherlands, the German states, Italy and Spain, ultimately united most of Europe against him in the War of the Spanish Succession, a conflict that was to spread over two continents, and set the pattern for the global struggles of our own century. But his unification and restructuring of France, his conversion of his kingdom, so to speak, into a kind of vast formal garden with great alleys leading directly into the glittering palace of Versailles, produced a simultaneous explosion in art, architecture and literature that made France seem a new Greece, to be emulated by all her neighbors. Louis XIV may have been, in the words of Winston Churchill, an international pest, but to many Frenchmen even today, more than any other figure in Gallic history he exemplified the ancient concept of *gloire*. For this some of them still tend to look away from his bloody, useless wars and the savage religious persecutions that sent thousands of his ablest subjects fleeing to other lands that were astute enough to welcome and make use of them.

The man we see in the portraits of Rigaud, with grave, glazed eyes and a splendid aquiline nose, a height magnified by high red heels and a perruque, could hardly remember a time when he had not been king. Rarely has a monarch more perfectly adapted mind and body to the demands of etiquette and rule. Louis was a living ceremonial; he seemed never to tire, never to need privacy. He was always king, God's representative on earth, whether on his throne, his steed, his privy or his mistress' bed. After the death of Cardinal Mazarin, when at twenty-three he assumed the reins of government, he would never have a prime minister. He had a council that tendered advice, but the final decision was always his, as was the ultimate responsibility both for the glory and the defeats. Even his bitterest critics could not deny that he played the role of absolute monarch with style and decorum. He was like a king in a legend: majestic, awesome, lofty. He delighted all that was theatrical in his subjects, and there was a good deal of that.

It is significant that we picture him on a solitary throne. There is never a queen beside him. He was married, it is true, for more than two decades to a Spanish infanta, Marie-Thé-rèse, but she was a colorless little thing who never shared his limelight. Then there were the mistresses, but of all of these only Madame de Montespan cut any figure in court, and even she had no political influence. Ultimately she was sent away. Madame de Maintenon he married, but the marriage was kept secret, and she was allowed to play the spouse only in her suite. Many observers felt that she, unlike the other favorites, did exercise some power in affairs of state, but most historians today do not think so. Louis detested the slightest female interference with his government. He might have raised his hat gallantly to a chambermaid, but he did not regard women as having a role to be noted in the serious business of life. The strides that women made toward emancipation in his reign were with no help from him.

I believe that he may have associated the civil wars of the Fronde in his boyhood, the memory of which he so violently detested, with the plottings of women. His mother, Anne of Austria, as regent had leaned heavily on Giulio Mazarini, the Italian known to history as Cardinal Mazarin, to help her rule, and the opposition of the great nobles to this wily foreigner had been aided and abetted by a group of remarkably forceful women: the duchesse de Longueville (a Bourbon and sister of the Grand Condé), the duchesse de Chevreuse, the princesse Palatine, the duchesse de Montbazon and Mlle. de Montpensier (known as la Grande Mademoiselle, Louis' own first cousin). Indeed, the Fronde has always been given a sort of *opéra-bouffe* treatment by historians, as if the "petticoat influence" of these ladies, intriguing in court and sometimes at the very front, had robbed the conflicts of the sober seriousness of purely man-made wars.

Although the government was headed by the queen mother, most of the women involved were rebels. The crown was directed toward absolute monarchy, and that meant curtailment of the power of the great nobles through whom these women derived their influence. The duchesse de Longueville organized the forces supporting her brother Condé; the duchesse de Chevreuse and Madame de Montbazon, on a less exalted level, carried on Dumasesque intrigues, and la Grande Mademoiselle turned the guns of the Bastille on the royal troops. But the greatest statesman among them was the princesse Palatine, an heiress to the duchy of Nevers, who had married a grandson of James I of England and who had the vision to see the ultimate futility of the rebellion and to come back to her old friend the queen mother to arrange the needed final peace.

These women caught the public imagination. They were energetic, handsome, given to romance. They were brave and proud and quarrelsome. And they were certainly no pettier than the men with whom and against whom they worked. It was becoming evident that they were as well equipped as males to deal with a government that was run by intrigue in palace corridors. Perhaps better.

Their example provided inspiration to the greatest poet of the day, Pierre Corneille, who proceeded to endow the female characters of his tragedies with the virile powers usually associated with warriors. The plays of this period ring with the high tones of their heroines. Émilie in *Cinna* offers to marry Cinna if he will assassinate Augustus; Cornélie, in *La Mort de Pompée*, released by an enemy whom she admits to be noble and generous, yet warns him that she will continue to seek his death; Théodore in *Théodore* joyfully embraces a martyr's death, happy to have been spared the worse fate of rape; Cléopâtre in *Rodogune* plots to keep her crown at the cost of murdering both her sons; Rodelinde in *Pertharite* disdains to save her infant's life at the price of marriage to her conqueror; Sophonisbe in *Sophonisbe* takes poison to avoid the shame of being led in triumph by Scipio; Aristie in *Sertorius* affirms that a sovereign queen should marry for political reasons alone, and Pulchérie in *Pulchérie* carries this one step farther by according her consort her hand but not her body.

It was not only in battle and in the court that women were making their influence felt; it was also in the salons. In Paris the marquise de Rambouillet had established her hôtel as a center for discussion of the arts and sciences. Molière made mock of the affectations and airs of this salon in his comedies *Les Précieuses Ridicules* and *Les Femmes Savantes,* but there was much genuine love of learning under the surface foolishness, and even Molière makes Philaminte, in the second of these plays, a person of considerable power who, armed with a philosophy at which the author sneers, is nonetheless able to face a threatened bankruptcy with equanimity. What one can see today in these plays is the opportunity that books offered to women, hitherto bound either to domestic servitude or the cloister, to operate on equal terms with the other sex. The women in the comedies may be foolish and misguided, but the deadening common sense of the playwright's spokesmen gives us a glimpse of how dreary was the role conventionally expected of them. Not everyone may have laughed with Molière at Armande when she exclaims:

"Loin d'être aux lois d'un homme en esclave asservie,
*Mariez-vous, ma soeur, à la philosophie!"**

Molière, after all, had never been a wife. The Hôtel de Rambouillet was a college that was to have distinguished graduates: Mesdames de La Fayette and de Sévigné.

It will be observed that I am constantly dealing in noble names. But in the seventeenth century, had these women not been born high in the social scale they would never have been heard of. It was not the time for self-made men or women. Even in war, the great commanders—Condé, Turenne, Vendôme, Villars, Berwick and Eugène of Savoy—were all born royal or noble, and Marlborough was the son of a knight. If men found it difficult to work their way up, what chance was there for women? The army, the church, the professions were frozen. In the arts there was more leeway, but how could a poor, ill-educated female get into these?

Besides the court and the world of letters, women had two other sources of influence: the church and the boudoir. Simultaneously with the emergence of women in the Fronde came the reform of the convents. The remarkable women of the Arnauld family led the way to a change of face in cloisters in

* "Instead of being a slave to the laws of men, wed yourself, sister, to philosophy!"

many parts of France, substituting for ease and laxness, and sometimes actual dissipation, an austere and ordered life of retirement and devotion. Such a reform may not seem so desirable to modern observers, but it was at least a protest against the indignity of depriving women of their sexual function without giving them any other. The epicurean convent was the ultimate debasement of the sex.

As to the boudoir, it would come into its own with the majority of Louis XIV and the re-establishment of absolute male authority. The great Frondeuses now found themselves in disfavor at court; Madame de Longueville retired to a convent, and la Grande Mademoiselle was sent to mope in her château in the country. The too serious sisters of the reformed convents at Port-Royal were accused of heresy and ordered to recant, and it became known that the king would tolerate no female interference in affairs of state. If a woman was to have any real voice in her own life, or in the life of the court, it would have to be by her own hold on men's senses. It was the day of the Mancini girls and, ultimately, of Madame de Montespan.

This setback to women in the middle years of Louis' reign was somewhat balanced by what occurred across the Channel. Because the Salic law, which excluded women from the French crown, did not obtain in England, the deposition of James II in 1688 was followed by the reigns of two queens regnant, his daughters Mary II and Anne. Mary II surrendered her authority to her husband, William III, but Anne maintained hers jealously. Indeed, her principal opponent in the wielding of it was another woman, the duchess of Marlborough. It was Anne, as we shall see, who first defeated Louis XIV and ultimately saved him, by bringing a halt to the war that she deemed to have been sufficiently won.

In the final years of Louis' reign there seem to have been only three persons, all women, who were trying to restore sanity to European affairs. Anne in England was working actively for peace; Madame de Maintenon, at Versailles, was working less obviously, but as hard as she dared, for the same objective, and the princesse des Ursins, adviser to Philip V in Madrid, though a thorough belligerent, was nonetheless passionately concerned with forging Spain into a strong state that would not be subject to the horror of constant invasions by foreign powers. These women were all working for a future where human beings might lead their lives in some kind of peace and order, free of border conflicts and religious dissension and liberated from the "glory" so popular to the public mind. The only other important person working for the same goal was Dean Swift, who had the sense to comprehend that Queen Anne was the key to everything that he wished to accomplish.

There were female contemporaries, of course, who were as blind as the men. Mary of Modena, the consort of James II of England, was as bigoted a Roman Catholic as the century could boast, and she used all of her considerable charm and ability in exile to head every plot to destroy the peace of Britain and place her son on the throne that his father had lost. Sarah Churchill, the duchess of Marlborough, would have carried on the War of the Spanish Succession until both sides were bled white; she would have turned Europe into a graveyard to assure the triumph of the Whigs. Indeed, it was thanks to such firebrands as she that France, rendered at last desperate by the harshness of the allied ultimatum, began to fight in 1709 with the spirit that she was to show a century later in 1792. The intense nationalism that grew out of a war that had started over tight dynastic questions was to be a grim legacy to posterity, and Mary of Modena and Sarah Churchill must bear their share of the responsibility for this.

But the prevailing voice of women was in favor of compromise. The Arnauld sisters may have resisted recantation, but they did not seek to impose their views on others. And there were women who were willing to work for peace in the church as well as between nations. Madame de Brinon was one of these. Madame de Maintenon had installed her as director of the girls' school at St. Cyr, but when she had found it politic to bow to ecclesiastical demands that only nuns be qualified for this position, Madame de Brinon became a protégée of the abbess of Maubuisson, sister of the electress Sophia of Hanover. Through the abbess' German relations, she entered into a learned correspondence with the philosopher Leibniz and conceived of a project no less grandiose than the reunification of the Catholic and Protestant churches. To bring this about she engaged Leibniz in a famous correspondence with Bossuet, Bishop of Meaux. These two mighty thinkers, after filling a volume with their weighty arguments about the interpretation of the Council of Trent, rumbled at last to an impasse and to a personal clash that brings to mind the animosities that follow the elaborate compliments between the two pedants in *Les Femmes Savantes*.

Madame de Brinon's letters, pleadingly interspersed amid the thunderbolts, read like the voice of reason in a storm. A century earlier Catherine de Médicis, making the same plea for religious reconciliation, had been accused by the papal legate of not knowing the meaning of the word "dogma." What chance did the practical common sense of well-meaning women have in a day when men backed intolerance? Here is one of Madame de Brinon's final pleas to Bossuet in 1693:

> Whatever happens, my Lord, do not allow our brothers [the Protestant churches] to escape us. Hold to the methods you have proposed, and let them set one foot in our manger; the other will follow soon enough. And, I beg of you, don't make them subscribe to the Council of Trent all at once. Even God does not accomplish his greatest works at one stroke. I am touched by the persistence with which these honest Protestants keep turning back to

us. We should be filled with the charity of Christ for
them—so long as no sacred truth is compromised. I
urge you in the name of God, my Lord, to give
yourself to this great task and make it work!

The death of Louis XIV in 1715 provided a delayed opening of the eighteenth century. It has often been claimed that
women dominated this so-called Age of Reason, and in some
ways they did, but I suspect that they did not do so to their
own ultimate advantage. I suggest that what women really
accomplished in the eighteenth century was to harness their
force and genius to the chariot of charm, and in so doing to
decorate the age with a grace that no age before or since has
been able to boast. But what was it, in fact, but decoration?
The eighteenth century may have been a women's century,
but it was also the century of Boucher and Fragonard.

The contrast between the reigns of the Sun King and of
Louis XV can be seen in the portraits of each era. In the
earlier we have splendid ladies attired in the garments of god-
desses with clouds swirling about them, perhaps with a leop-
ard skin over a shoulder and a bow and quiver in hand, fresh
from slaying some beast of legend; a Juno or a Minerva, or
sitting magnificently in a straight-backed chair, ready to receive a visiting potentate, before an open window through
which acres of formal gardens and alleys and fountains appear.
Their sisters of the later epoch are viewed under more beguil-
ing auspices, in sleds with pretty cupids as coachmen, or rising
from bed, with a sense of being spied upon, even by a gallant
disguised as a lady's maid, or bathing by a Hubert Robert
waterfall. So successful were the ladies of the court of the
"Well-Beloved," as Louis XV was fatuously known, that the
whole era bespeaks their accomplishment: we think of it as a
parlor with paneled walls and Lancret paintings and exquisite
porcelains, an interior that could be presided over only by a
very charming woman. And to some extent women may have

attained to a real power through good taste. Madame de Pompadour is the representative *par excellence* of the age: because she made a beautiful and amusing thing out of the boredom of Versailles, the king was willing to let her try her hand in international politics.

It all blew up, of course, in the French Revolution, to be succeeded by the long sobriety of the nineteenth century, as appropriately named for Victoria as the seventeenth was for Louis. Women had to start afresh. But I like to speculate that the suffragettes of the twentieth century picked up where Madame de Maintenon, the princesse des Ursins and good Queen Anne left off.

II
La Grande Mademoiselle

In 1670 Madame de Sévigné, writing of "Mademoiselle," the duchesse de Montpensier, and the latter's agony at the withdrawal of the king's consent to her marriage, describes her sympathy for her afflicted friend as more intense than "one usually feels for persons of that rank." This aptly expresses the loneliness of royalty in the seventeenth century and helps to explain the obtuseness in princes and princesses resulting from undeveloped imaginations.

"Mademoiselle," as the eldest daughter of the French king's brother was known, Anne-Marie-Louise d'Orléans, was born in 1627, doubly a Bourbon. Her father was Gaston, duc d'Orléans, heir presumptive to the still childless Louis XIII, and her mother was Marie de Bourbon, last of a younger line in the direct male descent from Saint Louis, who, dying in childbirth, left the baby girl a duchess in her own right and the richest heiress of Europe. Mademoiselle grew up into a big, blond, large-nosed, blue-eyed girl, dreadfully spoiled but good-natured, naïve and always basically decent. She considered her mother's mother, a mere duchess, as less closely related to her than her father's mother, Marie de Médicis, who was not only a queen, but the mother of a king and two queens. Yet she wondered a little if it might not be fatuous to make such distinctions. Mademoiselle was a bit of an ass, but she sometimes, if only dimly, suspected this. V. Sackville-West, one of her later biographers, has confessed that in the sad parts of Mademoiselle's story she felt the impulse to wipe away the big Amazon's tears.

For who cared about the little girl? Nobody. Her father, Gaston, who spent his adult life conspiring against the two cardinal-ministers who ran the French state, first Richelieu and then Mazarin, and who always escaped with his neck and properties intact by betraying his co-conspirators, may have reeked of infamy, but he had still enough charm to dazzle the child whose fortune he was busy embezzling. Her aunt, Anne of Austria, queen mother and regent during the minority of Louis XIV, was amiable enough, but only because she wanted to keep a wealthy niece on tap, in case of need and despite that niece's greater age, for her two small sons. And her other aunt, the exiled queen Henrietta-Maria of England, cultivated her with an eye to using her fortune to help Prince Charles recover his throne from Oliver Cromwell. And there was hardly a member of Mademoiselle's huge household who did not seek something from her. One is sure they robbed her blind.

She learned early that the world was bound to fawn and cheat. But she saw at the same time that flattery and cupidity were proof that she must have assets worth praising and stealing. If one had to be great, should one not be great with style? With gusto? If one's environment was always turning itself into a stage on which one seemed destined to play a major role, might one not perform better if one enjoyed it? Bring on the helmet, the spear, the steed! She would ride into battle to the sound of trumpets.

It was obvious to her that she was going to have to look out for herself. When she came of age, she was told that it would not be proper to ask an accounting of her father or her maternal grandmother. She was expected to sign releases without asking embarrassing questions. But she held them both to a strict responsibility, demanding enormous damages, and let her father off the hook only when serious pressure was applied by the royal family to make her do so. And when a proposed manager of her properties told her that he expected his clients to enjoy themselves and not bother him with questions about businesses that they could never understand, she got rid of him quickly. Mademoiselle was smart enough to understand, in business and later in war, that if there were men who knew a lot more than she did, there were also plenty who knew as little or less. A "daughter of France" did not have to leave everything to males just because she had been born a female.

As Mademoiselle owes her place in history to her role in the wars of the Fronde, some attention must be given to these. There were two of them, a brief one in 1648–49, and a longer one in 1651–53. They were civil wars, really more like feuds, in which the court party, headed by the young king and his regent mother and guided by Cardinal Mazarin, was opposed by a faction of great nobles and princes of the blood. The term *fronde* came from a slingshot used by boys in the streets of Paris. The name has been seized on by historians to justify a version of the war as semiserious, a kind of *opéra-bouffe* or masque where ladies and gentlemen played at sieges and forays, and where dancing and gallantry were substituted for drills.

Perhaps because the issues at stake were not grave historical ones like the burning of heretics or the looting of neighbors, these wars have been downgraded. Reading Mademoiselle's journal, one would suppose that trade and commerce and business did not exist, that history was made up of the quarrels within her own family. But perhaps Mademoiselle was right. Perhaps history *is* trivial. Perhaps the wars of the Fronde are unforgivable because they show so blatantly how silly wars in the seventeenth century could be.

The basic issue at stake was the authority of the crown. In

the first, brief war it was the *parlement* of Paris against the queen mother's unpopular minister. That was soon settled. The second was more serious, involving a deep cleavage in the royal family. Succession to the throne was limited to male descendants of a sovereign in the direct male line. The first two generations from a reigning king were known as sons and grandsons of France; the subsequent ones as "princes of the blood." In the second Fronde, the first prince of the blood, Louis de Bourbon, prince de Condé, called the Grand Condé, though only a third cousin of the boy king, was actually third in line to the throne, after the king's delicate younger brother, Philippe, and his elderly uncle, Gaston. This proximity to supreme power, plus Condé's vast wealth and domains (which included Burgundy, Berry and much of Lorraine), and the fact that, after Turenne, he was the ablest soldier in the land, gave him, at least in his own opinion, the right to dominate the council of the young monarch—certainly more so than an Italian adventurer of dubious birth whose oily tricks and sheep's eyes at the queen mother had made him a cardinal and a minister. Condé had been on the royal side in the first Fronde, but he and Gaston were disgusted at the continued sway of Mazarin and made their disgust a *casus belli.*

The war was complicated. Condé held Paris against the crown and allied himself with the Spaniards in the lowlands which were still at war with France. There was a good deal of side changing and genteel communication between the opposing forces. The forces of the "princes" always insisted, despite their foreign allies, that they were basically loyal to the king. They simply aimed to liberate the unfortunate youth from the wily cardinal. But despite the courtliness between the two armies there was plenty of bloody fighting before the king's party prevailed and established the absolute monarchy that would last till the Revolution.

Mademoiselle found herself in her element. Instead of being a placid pawn on the European marriage market—would she demean herself by marrying the penniless exiled prince of Wales?; was the widowed Emperor Ferdinand III too old?— she was able to assert herself as a power in her own right. Gaston was too scared and too tricky to commit himself to direct armed opposition to his nephew, so she went in his stead to Orléans, gained access to the town through an inadequately guarded gate and persuaded the good burghers to deny access to the royal army. Needless to say, she made the most she could of the obvious parallel to herself and the Maid of Orléans!

Back in Paris, where the royal troops were approaching the city, threatening to cut off and annihilate the retreating army of Condé, she saved him by turning the guns of the Bastille on the enemy and slaughtering a whole file of the royal cavalry, including, unfortunately for her, a nephew of Mazarin. It may have been her finest hour, but it was also the end of her dream of marrying the young sovereign, whose ultimate victory was still inevitable. Condé was saved, but it was only a matter of time before they all—Condé, Gaston and Mademoiselle herself—would have to make their peace with the queen and cardinal. Mademoiselle was punished by being made to languish for years in her country estates before returning to what all her contemporaries regarded as the only true bliss in life: the court.

Exile, anyway, gave her the opportunity to start her memoirs, which have made a lively and novel contribution to the history of her era. She makes a valiant effort in them to be candid about herself. She pinpoints her principal fault as generosity; it is this that has made her so often the dupe of designing folk. But she sees nothing wrong in great pride of birth and roundly asserts that, had she been born in a republic, she would have been a rebel. Even those friends who have taken her side against her treacherous father must not be allowed to criticize a son of France. And although she is distressed by the bloodshed of civil war, it never occurs to her

that she or Condé or her father could have been wrong.
When in Orléans, after commandeering the mail to seek out
treasonable correspondence and burning it, she regrets the
inconvenience to merchants, but it never crosses her mind
that the innocent letters could have been sent on. These people, after all, were of no importance compared to princes and
peers. It is fascinating to her readers today to speculate
whether she saw France as it was or whether she was creating
a fantasy.

It has been said that Mademoiselle was a caricature of a
Corneille heroine. But why a caricature? It seems to me that
she was a Corneille heroine to the life. People who know the
poet only in his greatest tragedies, *Le Cid*, *Horace* and
Polyeucte, are not aware of how odd he could be in his lesser
ones. His women in the latter, like Mademoiselle, are always
intoxicated with their exalted rank. They assign the highest
dignity to what is apt to strike us as the crassest kind of ambition, and they snipe at each other with a shrillness that
Voltaire found unworthy of tragic drama. Mademoiselle
might have exclaimed, like Viriate in *Sertorius*:

> "La liberté n'est rien quand tout le monde est libre,
> Mais il est beau de l'être, et voir tout l'univers
> Soupirer sous le joug, et gémir dans les fers."*

It is difficult for any but a Frenchman to believe that Corneille could ever have been taken seriously as a political
thinker, but he was. He defined *gloire* precisely, at least as I
see it: the thrill of trampling on one's neighbor for the pleasure of trampling. It was *gloire* that induced Louis XIV, year
after year, to send his splendid armies into Holland, Flanders
and the German states, plundering and slaughtering their
wretched populations without the slightest economic gain for
his own people. After fifty years of this France was left ex-

---

* "Liberty is nothing when all the world is free. But it is a fine thing to be free and
see the rest of the world groaning in chains."

hausted and worse off than in the beginning, but the Sun King no doubt had gained his *gloire.*

We can hardly blame Mademoiselle for being taken in by a doctrine that was passionately embraced by all the men and most of the women of her acquaintance. But the tragedy that awaited her in 1670 was less like one written by Corneille than by his younger rival, Racine, who had just produced a *Bérénice* far finer than the master's tragedy on the same subject. *Phèdre,* still seven years in the future, would have some of the agony of Mademoiselle's tragic episode, but none of its absurdity. For even Racine never made fun of *gloire.* Did he not give up the stage to become the Sun King's historiographer and accompany him on a military campaign?

At forty-three Mademoiselle was something rarely found in a European court: an old maid princess. She still believed that every unwed male royalty was casting eyes in her direction, but it is not likely that this was so. Propagation of the line was the first duty of a royal consort, and her age was hardly propitious. It seems equally improbable that the king would allow her wealth to leave France, and within the borders who was left? The king, his brother, the princes de Condé and de Conti were all wed. It is small wonder that Mademoiselle should have begun to ask herself if she had not reached an age when she might marry as she chose.

Probably this speculation followed, rather than preceded, her infatuation with Antonin de Caumont, duc de Lauzun, an eccentric but fascinating Gascon, an officer of the king's guard, five years her junior. He is a difficult man to understand, even though he is carefully described in the memoirs of the duc de Saint-Simon, whose wife's brother-in-law he later became. It seems possible that he was a little bit mad. Small and plain, although muscular and finely built, he had an insolent temper and a devastating wit that made him feared even by persons who greatly outranked him. Although an ambitious and assiduous courtier, he found it impossible to resist the temptation of a cutting remark, even when it was bound to upset the ladder that he had carefully placed against the social wall to be scaled. When he discovered, for example, that the king's mistress, Madame de Montespan, had double-crossed him in the matter of a requested favor, speaking against him rather than for him to the king—a fact which Lauzun had ascertained by actually hiding under her bed during a royal visit—he did not hesitate, on his next meeting with the favorite, to call her a bitch and a whore. Poor Mademoiselle was ultimately to be treated hardly less scathingly.

But not, of course, at first. It is perfectly obvious to anyone reading between the lines of her ingenuous account of their first meetings that Lauzun knew from the start that he had caught her fancy and was considering with the greatest care just what advantage he might glean from it. He pretends to be deaf to all her hints, and, when he agrees at last to advise her on the question of her marriage, he purports to find no suitor of appropriate rank. Mademoiselle, rebuffed and discouraged, decides to fight her infatuation as hard as she can, which is not very hard. Would it not be better at her age, she asks herself desperately, to marry a man whom she can help and who will owe everything to her, rather than some monarch who would take her rank and fortune for granted? But what about all those Corneille heroines and their passionate concern for rank? The poor woman now pores through the plays seeking excuses for herself. Did Lauzun not claim descent from ancient Scottish kings? Her friend Madame de Sévigné encouraged this delusion by quoting the master's lines in *Polyeucte:*

Je ne le puis du moins la blâmer d'un mauvais choix,
Polyeucte a du nom et sort du sang des rois. *

---

* At least I cannot blame her for an unworthy choice. Polyeucte has a good name, and his blood is royal.

Lauzun's quandary was a real one. If he were to marry Mademoiselle without the king's authority, he might spend the rest of his life in the Bastille. If they sought the royal permission, on the other hand, it might be granted only on condition that the match be secret and morganatic, in which case Lauzun might receive fewer honors and settlements than if he should marry an heiress (and a younger and prettier one at that) of his own rank. Besides, was there not something ridiculous for a man of his many romantic liaisons with great ladies of fashion to become the puppet husband of a silly, infatuated old maid, a head taller than himself, even if she was a granddaughter of France? But there was still another possibility. Suppose he were to play his hand—and, after all, he was on friendly terms with the king—so as to win a grand slam: marry Mademoiselle with the blessing of his master and become duc de Montpensier and the richest peer in France?

It was worth a gamble. The greatest caution would have to be used with all concerned, particularly Mademoiselle. He would have to make it appear that the marriage was entirely *her* idea, that he had never dared raise eyes to the king's cousin until he had begun to fear that her passion might drive her to some desperate or unseemly step.

He continued his policy of pretending not to understand her hints of love until he had forced her to a written declaration. He then took the position that it was some kind of a joke, that she was trying to make a fool of him, that she must know it was her plain duty to marry the recently widowed "Monsieur," the king's brother, who had inherited her father's style and title, or even her cousin, the young duc de Longueville. There is a pathetic picture in the memoirs of Mademoiselle, trembling with the double chill of the weather and of her beloved's response, falling to her knees to warm herself by the fire, while the odiously respectful Lauzun, standing by her side, murmurs in her ear that he is more paralyzed by what she is trying to tell him than she is by the cold. And then he would excite her and torment her at once by assuring her that if he ever married, it would not be for riches or rank, but only for virtue, that even a position such as hers would be no temptation to him without love!

When Mademoiselle had been sufficiently pulverized and her passion for him finally acknowledged, and when it was certain that Monsieur, the duc d'Orléans, would not seek her as a second spouse, Lauzun decided that it was at last time to petition for the king's consent. Of course Mademoiselle had to write the letter, but we can be sure that he weighed its every phrase. The king, after reading it, returned word that he was "somewhat surprised." Obviously he was aware of Mademoiselle's infatuation—everyone at court was. But he simply advised her to think it over carefully, and when she waited until two the next morning to tell him that she had done so, coming to him as he rose at last from the gambling table, he told her that she was old enough to do as she wanted and refused either to give his consent or withhold it. It looked as if he were actually going to leave the matter to her and Lauzun!

Of course, they should have been married immediately. They shouldn't have wasted a minute. Madame de Sévigné saw this and urged her friend to act at once. The king himself was to say the same thing—later. But Mademoiselle could not believe that he would go back on his stated neutrality, and Lauzun hoped to obtain more by awaiting the formal blessing. When the duc de Montausier, in forcible terms, begged them both to hurry the matter, Lauzun stood silently by, examining his fiancée's miniatures. "Do you want to collect paintings or do you want to get married?" his disregarded counselor angrily exclaimed. Mademoiselle's memoirs in this tense period make painful reading. She is excited, euphoric, even occasionally jealous. Her head is full of daydreams. She sets forth in detail the chimerical claims of the Lauzun family to royal connections; she probes ancient history to find examples of French princesses marrying men of lesser stature. Had not the daughters of Dagobert wed nobodies?

This precious time was not wasted by the opposition. The queen, the tiny Marie-Thérèse, the Spanish infanta who was her husband's double first cousin (they shared all four grandparents), may have had a mind and an imagination as small as her figure, but she could be very fierce about the few areas that concerned her: her rank, her soul's salvation and the establishment of her younger son (who died early). She wanted Mademoiselle's inheritance for little Anjou, and she made no bones about it. Philippe, the king's brother, wanted this inheritance for himself, but he and his sister-in-law were at least united in their sincere horror of the contamination of the blood royal by the proposed alliance. In this they were joined by the other members of the royal family and by many of the great nobles. Had bloody civil wars been fought, had Richelieu and Mazarin devoted all their political lives to establish the supremacy of the crown only to have a Gascon adventurer like Lauzun *cousiner* with the king?

Louis XIV was on the spot. Like many aristocrats he would have liked to be exempt from his own laws, but he had enough political wisdom to sense that an exception so glaring to the quasi-divine status of the royal family might not be one to prove the rule, but one to prove its destruction. It was hardly feasible, after all, to maintain the divine right of kings if one did not respect one's own divinity, and it was certainly not a mark of respect to accord one's cousin-german, a princess with a double share of Bourbon blood, to a mere gentleman of the guard. It was a sticky business, for Louis was fond of his addlepated, elderly cousin, despite her long-forgiven broadside from the Bastille, and he bitterly regretted having fed her false hopes, but he was not a man to shirk a scene, and he had the moral courage to tell Mademoiselle the bad news to her face. They even embraced and shed tears together. Had he not as a youth given up Marie Mancini?

The king was to be sorely tempted again, later in his reign, to betray the same principle, but he resisted it. No historian to this day can prove that he was actually married to Madame de Maintenon. Not only was there no idea of making her queen, she was not raised higher than a marquise; and although she was accorded the position of a consort in the privacy of her rooms and of the royal family, in court she took only her given rank. With his bastards by Vallière and Montespan he strained the principle much more roughly, but he never entirely broke it. They were legitimated and married to princes of the blood, and the duc du Maine and the comte de Toulouse were actually placed in the line of succession to the throne, but this was made contingent upon the extinction of *all* issue in the direct male line from Hugues Capat, and it was swept away by the *parlement* soon after the old king's demise, as he had told them all along it would be. Only old age and the constant nagging of Madame de Maintenon, Maine's adoring former governess, had made him go as far as he had.

It was bad enough for Mademoiselle to have her marriage banned, but far worse was to follow. The king, perhaps correctly, fearing a counterstroke by the notoriously daring Lauzun, suddenly had him arrested and incarcerated in the château de Pignerol in Savoy. Nor was this the comfortable incarceration, with many servants and a good kitchen, meted out to some of the nobles who fell into royal disfavor. It was durance vile, under heavy guard, in small chambers with a minimum of books and writing material, and it lasted for ten long years. What could possibly have justified the king to his own mind in so treating a subject who had been guilty of no alleged crime? It is possible, of course, that Louis did not know how rough the treatment was. Certainly, having been a sovereign from the age of four, he found it difficult to put himself in Lauzun's position. But it is also true that he had his distraught cousin constantly before his eyes. For all the tears that he had once shed with her, he must have been a fairly heartless man.

Whatever can be said in defense of the locking up of Lauzun, nothing can be said in defense of the method of his enfranchisement. For when Mademoiselle was in her fifties, an age when an inappropriate marriage, secret or otherwise, would have been more ridiculous than dangerous (Madame de Sévigné writes that her friend has at last given up dancing, "thank God!"), the king and Madame de Montespan sold her Lauzun's liberty in return for a huge settlement on their son, the duc du Maine. Louis XIV had descended a step below Winston Churchill's rank for him of "pest." He was now an extortioner.

Mademoiselle tells us in her memoirs just how this was done. For some time she had made a habit of calling daily on Madame de Montespan, who professed a great sympathy for the desolate captive. One day she went further and suggested to Mademoiselle that she should consider how best to please the king if she really wished to obtain her heart's desire. There were others to carry this hint forward, and Mademoiselle found herself encouraged now to visit the royal bastards, particularly the pretty little duc du Maine. She at last nerved herself to suggest to Madame de Montespan that she would make Maine her heir in return for the liberty of Lauzun and a royal consent to their marriage. The favorite, who could be totally charming when she wished to be and who chose now to dazzle poor Mademoiselle, cautioned her that it was a mistake to try to bargain with the king. One should simply offer all and depend on his goodness. When Mademoiselle ventured to demur, the favorite's tone abruptly changed. One must not quibble with the king! If Mademoiselle did not deed the sovereignties of Dombes and Eu to Maine, Lauzun might find himself even more strictly incarcerated. Poor Mademoiselle collapsed and gave in, and the Montespan was immediately more lovely than ever. But that night the tortured princess broke a mirror by accident and regarded it as an unhappy augury.

It was. The king liberated Lauzun but allowed him to come only as near to Paris as Bourbon. There was no talk of consent to a marriage; any union would have to be secret. When Mademoiselle protested in a flood of tears, the favorite retorted coolly that she found her very difficult to please. The more Mademoiselle had, the more she wanted! "The king told me to tell you you must never think of a public marriage. Did I ever *promise* you anything?" Can't one hear her? Mademoiselle sobbed and raved, protesting that Madame de Montespan would have been kinder to have told her the harsh truth from the beginning. Even then she did not seem to realize how outrageously she had been duped. Madame de Montespan finally had the sense to placate the old girl a bit. Though she hated walking, she strolled that day in the gardens of St. Germain as long as Mademoiselle wanted, "without once complaining." It was a small price to pay for Dombes and Eu, and Madame de Montespan was always willing to pay a small price. The king was stingier; he would pay nothing.

Lauzun was at length allowed to return to court and Mademoiselle to see him, but it was all too late and too sour. He hated her now for the ruin of his life and career. The wealth she had bestowed on him was as nothing to the fact that he had lost the favor of the king and ten of the best years of his life. His terrible temper was even worse. He accused Mademoiselle of everything, from dowdiness of dress to personal extravagance. He even claimed that he would have got out of prison earlier without her interference, which was too much for Madame de Montespan, who roughly told him that he would have rotted in jail forever without the help of the princess. The favorite was capable of a certain good-natured fairness to others after she had feathered her own nest at their expense.

Lauzun became at length absolutely impossible. Mademoiselle had to close her doors to him. She may have secretly married him, but there is no evidence of such a union, and I find it difficult to believe that Lauzun would have risked the king's displeasure and a possible second imprisonment. Besides, he detested Mademoiselle. What is pathetic about the last few years of her life is that both she and Lauzun continued to curry the favor of the monarch who had caused them all their misery.

Nothing could better illustrate the godlike quality of Louis XIV in the eyes of his subjects. For a god did not have to be just or compassionate. He was God. There was no escaping the Sun King except in the hated dark. Like Job, the unhappy underling could only worship the hand that persecuted him. Mademoiselle was once again on good terms with the king and Madame de Montespan. Why not? They had everything they wanted from her. They even professed to seek her opinion on the marriage of the duc du Maine. She was, after all, the oldest member of the royal family. The last sentence in her memoirs, which break off abruptly in 1688, five years before her death at sixty-five, is that of the perennial courtier: "One day as I walked in the park at Versailles, I encountered the king; he stopped to speak to me . . ." What was left but heaven?

She bequeathed her wealth and domains, still vast despite the forced gift to Maine, to Monsieur, the king's brother. It was this inheritance that made the Orléans line so rich, right down to the Revolution, and enabled them so effectively to oppose the senior branch of the family. The Frondeuse in Mademoiselle had a posthumous revival after a lifetime of submission. In 1793 a duc d'Orléans would cast his vote for the execution of a king of France. The *opéra-bouffe* was over.

As for Lauzun, he donned deep mourning for his ex-fiancée, giving credence, no doubt intentionally now that it was safe, to rumors that he had actually married her. He had finally been made a duke, at the behest not of Mademoiselle but of the exiled James II whose wife he had helped to flee from England, and he lived to be ninety, rich and feared. One is not much saddened to learn that his child bride caused him agonies of jealousy.

III
Madame de La Fayette

The author of the only novel of the reign of Louis XIV that can still be read with profit and pleasure is so linked, both as woman and as artist, with that of the duc de La Rochefoucauld, author of the famous maxims, that the editors of Sainte-Beuve's *Portraits de Femmes* elected to include his portrait in it. And La Rochefoucauld's own earlier life as a warrior and Frondeur is so tied to that of the duchesse de Longueville that any study of Madame de La Fayette becomes something of a triangle.

Marie-Madeleine Pioche de La Vergne was born of humbler origin than her friends in the great world. Her father had been a mere *écuyer* or squire of the minor nobility, who had risen to be governor of the young marquis de Brézé, a nephew of Cardinal Richelieu. But it was not until 1650, when Marie-Madeleine was sixteen, that her widowed mother moved into the higher ranks by marrying Renaud-René de Sévigné, uncle by marriage of the letter writer who became her new stepcousin's lifelong friend.

Marie-Madeleine, even as a girl, was of a sober and religious disposition. She cultivated the discreet company of the sisters of the Couvent de Chaillot and became a protégée of Mère Angélique, the former Mademoiselle de La Fayette, who had been the object of the chaste passion of Louis XIII. Two important events stemmed from this. The first was Marie-Madeleine's arranged marriage with Mère Angélique's brother, the comte de La Fayette, twice his bride's age but a great catch in view of her small dowry. The second was her friendship with the exiled princess Henriette of England, daughter of the martyred Charles I, who lived with her mother, the dowager Henrietta-Maria, sister of Louis XIII, in the convent of her uncle's old flame. Henriette was then only ten and seemed a poor little thing of few prospects, but she was to grow up into the loveliest princess of her time and to marry, after her brother's restoration, Louis XIV's brother, the duc d'Orléans. She would be Madame de La Fayette's introduction to a court that would provide her with the basic source material of her fiction.

The Comte and Comtesse de La Fayette were married for many years and had children, but there seems to have been no real congeniality between them, and he was apparently contented to pass most of his time at his château in the Auvergne, absorbed in the extensive litigation so dear to provincial life of the day, leaving his wife in Paris in the company of her literary friends. Madame de La Fayette soon established a reputation as an intellectual, perhaps even as a *précieuse*. One of the intimates of her salon was the Abbé Ménage, supposedly a model used by Molière for Vadius, the pedant in *Les Femmes Savantes* who would ask of any man introduced to him: "Is he a Hellenist?"

The princess Henriette, "Minette," now duchesse d'Orléans and known as "Madame," wanted her old friend constantly at court with her. Madame's life was not an easy one. She had developed from a slip of a girl, a handful of bones in the contemptuous phrase of the young Louis XIV, into an enchanting creature, still very slight and thin, almost diaphanous, but with a haunting air of loveliness that charmed everyone, including her formerly critical brother-in-law, Louis. Unfortunately her husband, Monsieur, a pederast who was yet jealous of her effect on other men, treated her waspishly, though keeping her constantly pregnant out of a dreary sense of dynastic duty. It was said that he made love to her with the supposed aid of holy medals attached to his private parts. Madame had to use all her tact and subtlety to keep peace among the powerful courtiers who vied for her attention. This might not have been so difficult had she not chosen to have affairs, or at least serious flirtations, with several of them. But, poor creature, she had to have some fun. And she had the wit and humor, added to her native taste and intelligence, to be able to make a vivid drama of her intrigues and adventures, and to share it with her older and soberer friend, urging the latter to put it in a book.

It is difficult to get any very definite picture of Madame. Her portraits agree only in depicting a woman of no particular beauty. This quality, on which so many observers agree, must have emanated from her manner. That she was intelligent is certain, for the French Government used her as a special ambassador in its dealing with her brother, Charles II, who seems to have cared for her more than he did for any of his mistresses. Perhaps we see her best in the character of Mary, Queen of Scots, in Madame de La Fayette's historical novel *La Princesse de Clèves*, described at the time that Mary was married to the heir to the French crown and known by the lovely title *la reine-dauphine*.

Mary Stuart, like Madame, was popular and clever, the central female figure of a brilliant court, but she had always to reckon with powerful enemies ready to take advantage of her least misstep. Did this add to the fun? Possibly. She was determined not to be cheated of all the pleasures of life and love. And yet at times the game must have seemed hardly worth the candle. Perhaps it was a relief when the death of her boy husband sent her off to the bleak shores of Scotland.

Madame de La Fayette told Madame's story more literally

in her *Histoire de Madame Henriette d'Angleterre.* There the reader traces, at times almost tediously, the web of intrigue and spying and backbiting that grew up like a black thicket about the smallest gallantry permitted herself by a French princess. Whom could the poor girl trust? One man might love her for ambition, and that was bad enough, but it was almost worse when another loved her truly, for in the agony of his frustration and jealousy he might ruin her by indiscretion. Madame was watched by all, including her jealous sister-in-law Queen Marie-Thérèse, her suspicious mother-in-law Queen Anne, her husband, who resented the king's use of her in state matters, and her husband's homosexual lovers, who feared her influence on the man they sought to dominate. Madame seems to flit through the dark passageways of the Louvre and St. Germain, a brief vision of loveliness in a kind of seventeenth-century *Perils of Pauline.*

It all ended early, in 1670, when she was suddenly stricken with ghastly stomach pains and died in a few hours, crying out that she had been poisoned. Every student of French litera-ture knows the lament of Bossuet's great funeral oration: *"Madame se meurt! Madame est morte!"* Was she poisoned? Most of her contemporaries believed so, but they believed it of almost every royal death. Louis XIV, at any rate, according to Saint-Simon, was much relieved, many years later, when he discovered evidence that exculpated his brother of any share in the crime—if crime there was.

Madame de La Fayette's health had always been frail, and with the disappearance of her brilliant friend she gave up the court and devoted herself to a religious and literary life in Paris. This was the period of her close friendship, which might have been a love affair or simply an *amitié amoureuse,* with the duc de La Rochefoucauld, many years her senior, semiinvalided by gout and half blind. It was also the period in which she wrote *La Princesse de Clèves.*

Sainte-Beuve maintained that Madame de La Fayette's life

could be contained in three documents: a letter that she wrote to Madame de Sablé about a visit she received from the comte de Saint-Paul, reputedly the natural son of La Rochefoucauld; *La Princesse de Clèves;* and a letter of religious instruction written to her near the end of her life by her spiritual director, Du Guet. In the first of these documents she begs Madame de Sablé to persuade the young man that what he may have heard about herself and La Rochefoucauld is not the truth of their relationship. What she minds—and this is why I think Sainte-Beuve considers the letter so revealing—is not so much the fact of the affair (if indeed it was that) as her notion of how it might appear to youthful eyes. For how could a young soldier in his prime not see as either ridiculous or even as actually repellent a physical union between a man of his father's age and condition and a tall, grave female approaching forty? Madame de La Fayette believed that the body existed only as a temporary home for the soul, but she nonetheless wanted that home to be as lovely as possible. Her trouble lay in an underlying Jansenism (or puritanism) that caused her to suspect that any preoccupation with the decoration of that home was a source of evil and a distraction from God.

Certainly the external beauty of life at court informs every page of *La Princesse de Clèves.* The novel is placed in the reign of Henri II; the glittering magnificence of the Valois, like a diamond bracelet on black velvet, outshines their cruelty and decadence. The women are all beautiful and gorgeously attired; the men are all brave, handsome and equally gorgeous; they move slowly through the murky atmosphere of tournaments, dancing and gallantry, in vast Renaissance châteaux, like fantastic beetles. But what keeps the tone free of anything shiny or vulgar is the purity and simplicity of the prose. As in Racine the vocabulary is small, the descriptions are general rather than particular, and the effect is intensified by concentration and understatement.

A court whose people have nothing to do but intrigue for

power and commit adultery forms the setting for one perfect passion perfectly restrained: that of the beautiful young princesse de Clèves, wed to a man whom she deeply reveres but does not love, for the most accomplished gentleman and gallant warrior in the kingdom, the duc de Nemours. So violent is their mutual attraction, though scarcely articulated, that the princess confesses it to her husband and begs to be taken from court to avoid temptation. He insists that she remain and that he will trust her, but Nemours, who (most improbably) has overheard the confession, is now bent on pursuing her, if only with mute, beseeching glances, and Clèves, convinced at last that his wife has fallen, dies of a fever. The stricken heroine retires to a religious life, and Nemours, in the course of time, is cured of his passion.

The princesse de Clèves is more than the heroine; she is really the book itself. The contrast of her passion and her self-control make her a unique rose in the Valois garden. For everyone else is flawed: Clèves is consumed with jealousy and a rather unworthy curiosity; even Nemours, it is hinted, is naturally inconstant; the durability of his passion has been caused largely by the toughness of the obstacles to it. And the beautiful Mary of Scotland, however enchanting and sympathetic, is up to her ears in court gossip and gallantries.

But just what *is* the passion experienced by the princesse de Clèves? There is certainly little joy in it. It is all tears and shame. Even when she is free to wed as a widow, she is held back by more than a sense of guilt over her husband's death. She can never convince herself that she could hold the affections of Nemours after marriage, and she foresees a hell of jealousy. Love may be the only thing of any value in the world, but love is a snare and a delusion. It never lasts except when it is a source of pain to its possessor, as in the cases of both the heroine and her husband. It seems that the author is here guiding her heroine to the mystic position that there is nothing but vanity outside of God. But she makes her novel poignant by beautifully shaping the world that her heroine rejects.

The story was written in the years of Madame de La Fayette's friendship with La Rochefoucauld. Sainte-Beuve dated this friendship after 1665, the publication year of the latter's maxims, on the theory that the mollifying influence of this mutually inspiring relationship would have softened their cynicism. But I find this a sentimental argument. Sainte-Beuve could, on occasion, drip with sentiment. I do not believe that La Rochefoucauld would have changed the meaning of a single maxim because of Madame de La Fayette, though he would have, and undoubtedly did, adopt some of her suggestions for rephrasing. They worked together, like Walter Berry and Edith Wharton in the Paris of a later time. I do not imply by this that La Rochefoucauld was a co-author of *La Princesse de Clèves*. But I strongly suspect that he went over it with her, chapter by chapter, and that he not only corrected and edited the language, but suggested whole scenes and episodes. Something, anyway, happened to make this novel the sole masterpiece of her work.

La Rochefoucauld, as Sainte-Beuve well puts it, was all his life at heart a writer. Even at his most active—and he was very active indeed, as a conspirator, politician and warrior—there was something in his nature that held back, that wanted to stand aside to watch and comment, either on the beauty or on the futility of what was observed. As a young man in the era of Louis XIII and Richelieu, he had adopted the cause of the beautiful, neglected queen who dabbled in treason with her Spanish kin with the dash and enthusiasm of a hero of Dumas or Stanley J. Weyman, and had even plotted to abduct her and carry her beyond the cardinal's control. He had been plunged into the Bastille for his pains, but he had looked for his reward in the next reign, when Anne of Austria should be regent for her infant son. The queen mother, however, when that time came, fell—though this time quite voluntarily—

under the influence of another cardinal, Mazarin, and La Rochefoucauld, in disgust and self-interest, joined the party of the princes and made war on the minister.

The princes were the prince de Condé and his younger brother, the prince de Conti, third cousins to the king, but as previously pointed out, close to the succession and immensely rich in money and fiefs. Their sister, Anne Geneviève, was married to the much older duc de Longueville from whom she lived largely apart, preferring the life of power politics and gallantry that she found in the courts of her brothers, both of whom were devoted (some said incestuously) to her. It was this princess to whom the now cynical and embittered La Rochefoucauld resolved, quite deliberately and despite the existence of a wife and a large family, to attach his fortunes and what he still possessed of a heart.

Madame de Longueville is almost more a literary than a political figure, for French historians—certainly Sainte-Beuve and, even to an almost ridiculous extent, Victor Cousin— have tended to fall in love with her. She was blond, beautiful, frank and direct in her manners, a touch naïve, very brave, a loyal friend and (for the most part) a faithful lover, and she obviously radiated charm. It was not the subtle, touching charm of Madame, but it was perhaps more appropriate to the tumult of civil conflict. Cousin makes an icy villain out of La Rochefoucauld, which is probably exaggerated. He was certainly cool and calculating at the start of the affair, but there is evidence that he became genuinely devoted to his duchess, and she was certainly at least once unfaithful to him. It is amusing to note the horror and outrage with which her enthusiasts of two centuries later greet the ancient rumors that she may have been guilty not only of incest but of body odor. But I think all can agree that she was fascinating and that she had a generous heart.

La Rochefoucauld was hideously wounded in Paris during an assault of the royal troops on the town; Mademoiselle de

Montpensier saw him with an eye dangling. He was left largely blind in the long, anticlimactic aftermath of the Fronde. Madame de Longueville retired to Port-Royal for a penitence that lasted until her death in the same year, 1680, as her former lover. She ended a long written confession to her spiritual director on the note of a La Rochefoucauld maxim, admitting that her pleasure in writing at such length about her own sins might have been further evidence of the egotism that had dominated her life. But she seems not to have confined herself to that preoccupation with her own soul that obsessed so many noble penitents of her day. She engaged herself actively in the relief of areas that had been devastated in the wars of the Fronde, for which she held herself in some part responsible.

La Rochefoucauld, with poor sight and painful gout, led a life of semiretirement from the world, seeing a small number of close friends and polishing and repolishing the beautiful maxims that wryly summed up the tale of his disenchantment with his fellow men. One has only to contrast them with Sainte-Beuve's efforts in emulation to see how good they really are. One is surprised, actually, to find the few exceptions. It seems odd that the author of such brilliant comments as "We all have the fortitude to bear up under the misfortunes of our dearest friends," or "Every man complains of his memory; none, of his judgment," or "Hypocrisy is the tribute vice renders to virtue," should have included one as flat as "Fortune turns everything to the advantage of her favorites." But maxims must be judged individually, even when they form so decorative a unit as these. Reading them together is like strolling down some splendid gallery, a *salle des glaces* as at Versailles, and seeing ourselves in seventeenth-century mirrors.

He does not strike us, as he did his readers in the past, as such a misanthropist. That what he calls *amour-propre*, which might be translated as self-love, should be at the root of all human motivation seems obvious to those who have lived after Freud. The maxims apply as much to us as they did to their author's contemporaries, except for those concerned with coquetry in women—no longer the only weapon in the barren arsenal of a kept-down sex—and some of those dealing with court life. "A bourgeois manner may be shed in a soldier's life, never in a courtier's" has little application to a day of blurred class distinctions, but we know exactly what he means.

Madame de La Fayette was broken up by his death and survived him for only three years, which were largely devoted to religion. She seems at this point to have moved to the extreme mystic position that she had been approaching most of her life. The stern Du Guet, her director, remorselessly analyzed her past to persuade her that even her seemingly finest moments had been made up of illusion and vanity. It was as if La Rochefoucauld had returned to show her her life in maxims exhibiting her own self-love, with only the difference, no doubt a redeeming one to her, that faith would make up for the loss of all pleasure in life. Madame de La Fayette came to believe in the end that wisdom without God was nothing but good taste. One had to give up *all* the world to be saved, to let the beauty go with the ugliness. Even the *Princesse de Clèves*.

IV
Madame de Sévigné

My difficulty in reading the letters of Madame de Sévigné is that the French editions all contain either too many of them or too few. Letters do not generally lend themselves to selection. If they constitute a true correspondence and not a mere exchange of essays, their value will consist largely in their continuity, in the sense that they convey of a life or lives unrolling in a sequence of intimate, closely spaced scenes. But the trouble with reading Madame de Sévigné in a bulk of some dozen or more hefty tomes is that one tends to bog down in details of household chores and estate administration and in endless inquiries and responses about health. Not everyone has those fifteen rainy days in the country that Sainte-Beuve recommends for a complete perusal of the correspondence. On the other hand, if we confine ourselves to chosen excerpts—glimpses of court life, anecdotes about friends and relatives, witty and philosophical reflections about public events—we are reduced to a simple anthology of first-class reporting.

The best compromise seems to be to read her in a complete edition and to be prepared to do one's own skipping. It has been suggested that Madame de Sévigné wrote her letters with an eye to ultimate publication, but I do not for a minute believe that. It is true that she was understandably proud of them and pleased when she heard that they were being passed around among her friends and called for at social gatherings. But this, for the great lady that she was, was perhaps adequate publication, without what might have struck her as the vulgarity of print. Had she expected to see her letters ranged in volumes, as they posthumously were, she would certainly have pruned them of some of the duller details and repetitions. She was too much an artist not to have been tempted to cut out the gems of anecdote that sparkle like stars in a sometimes filmy sky. But then, of course, they would have ceased to be letters! No, we must take them as they are and be grateful.

The vast majority are addressed to her adored daughter, Françoise, wife of the Comte de Grignan, lieutenant governor of Provence. Françoise's letters are missing, having probably been destroyed by their diffident composer when she got them back from her mother's estate. It is an open question as to whether we are better or worse off without these. Surviving epistles from Madame de Grignan to other persons do not show the felicity of style about which her proud parent is always exclaiming. And Madame de Sévigné, like a monologist who has constantly to be repeating what her unseen colloquist is saying, is always helpfully summarizing what her daughter has just written. Perhaps it is as well that we are left with the great letter writer alone, with nothing to jar the flow of what amounts to a kind of epistolary journal.

She was born Marie de Rabutin-Chantal, in 1626, of a noble and affluent family, and was married at eighteen to the marquis de Sévigné, an attractive but dissipated young aristocrat who was killed in a duel over another woman, leaving her a beautiful young widow with two children, a boy and a girl, and a substantial but encumbered property. She chose never to remarry, or even, so far as one can make out, to engage in any pronounced gallantries, though some were naturally alleged. She undoubtedly flirted, but it was a day when widows had to be careful, and she was discreet.

The passion of her life was her beautiful daughter, and her reluctance to remarry, or even to love again, seems to have been motivated more by the fear of jeopardizing that daughter's establishment in the great world than by any great devotion to the memory of her scamp of a husband. She labored to make her farms in Brittany and Burgundy pay off, and she succeeded. Françoise was married, late but advantageously, to the comte de Grignan, a plain, older man, twice widowed and extravagant beyond his means, but nonetheless lieutenant governor of Provence and a sufficiently great personage. Françoise went south to live, thus giving rise to the long correspondence that was to make her adoring mother immortal.

It was natural enough that a young widow, solicitous to settle her children, should not have wanted to rock any political boats, and Madame de Sévigné was understandably conservative, but during the wars of the Fronde she had found herself in close relations with many powerful persons who were in opposition to the government. Of course, no one could then tell which side was going to prevail. But as a friend of such *Frondeurs* as the duc de La Rochefoucauld and la Grande Mademoiselle, she must have had a faint whiff of the rebel about her in the early years of Louis XIV's absolute authority, and this could not have been helped by her close friendship with Fouquet, the king's powerful finance minister who was disgraced and imprisoned on charges of treason, but really because he had presumed to rival the Sun King in his life style at Vaux-le-Vicomte. And still later in the reign Madame de Sévigné did not scruple to have many Jansenist friends, a sect that was anathema to the king.

Yet for all of this, no stronger supporter of the Sun King, even with all his wars and persecutions, existed than the indefatigable correspondent of the Hôtel Carnavalet and the château of Les Rochers. She cheered when the troops went off to

plunder Germany and the Lowlands; she noted every victory
with elation and minimized every defeat; she was impressed
by the royal mistresses and tolerant of royal adultery; she considered the splendor of the court a necessary expression of the
greatness of France. Hear her on her return from a first visit to
the now almost completed Versailles:

> I'm just back from Versailles; I have seen the beauti-
> ful apartments, and I am utterly charmed. If I had
> read it all in a novel, I should have called it a castle
> in Spain. But I've seen it and touched it; it is an
> enchantment but not an illusion. Everything is no-
> ble and fine, and the music and the dancing are
> sheer perfection. But what delighted me most was
> the privilege of living four hours with our sovereign,
> of being part, so to speak, of his pleasures, as he
> becomes a part of ours. It provides all that his loving
> subjects could wish: the joy of contemplating their
> master.

How to explain this seeming contradiction between independence of mind and hero worship? I think it was simply
that Madame de Sévigné had adapted herself as best she
could to the arbitrary contemporary world of male power. It
was not necessary for the king to be right or wrong. Like God,
he was there. Madame de Sévigné accepted the universe as
she found it. People had to be policed and ruled, and those
who had to do the policing and ruling could not be expected
always to be very delicate about it. Where she remained a
greathearted soul, however, was in never refusing her sympathy to friends who fell into royal disfavor. She might decline
to utter a word critical of the regime; she might not have felt
even much tempted to do so, but the victims, like the minister Fouquet and later the marquis de Pomponne, she treated
with open love and concern. She did not bewail the injustice
of their lot so much as its pitiableness. They might have been

the victims of a plague. One wept, one offered succor; one did not shake one's fist.

Her literary training began in the days of the salon of Madame de Rambouillet and the *précieuses.* The latter have been rendered ridiculous for all time by Molière, and undoubtedly they were guilty of absurd affectations, but there are two important reservations to note. In the first place, much of the preciosity may have covered a sincere concern with articulation, a desire to preserve and develop the finest parts of a language that was peerless for its exact and beautiful expression. And secondly, the role of the *précieuse* offered a rare, if not a unique opportunity for a woman to be something more than an inadequately educated virgin yanked out of a convent at a tender age to be matched with a stranger who was like as not a brute and who would abandon her for wars and duels and other women. Madame de Sévigné had a weapon in her pen that would make her the equal of any warrior of the time.

In the days of the Fronde she had seen women of her class playing more important roles than was customary for their sex: Madame de Longueville, the duchesse de Chevreuse, the princesse de Condé and la Grande Mademoiselle. These great ladies had been active in anti-government politics and even had taken part in battles. But when order had been restored and Louis XIV's power made absolute, they had faded from the political scene. Nothing in their fate seemed designed to make Madame de Sévigné discontented with her less martial role of letter writing.

Her acceptance of the brutalities of the age has been made much of by some commentators. But we probably daily condone actions that will seem cruel and inhuman to our posterity. Madame de Sévigné was a close friend of the governor of Brittany who put down a local rebellion with the usual ferocity. There is something chilling, to be sure, about her casual references to the hanging and quartering that he ordered, but that was the way those matters were handled, not only in

France but all over Europe. Even in the New World the set-
tlers were hanging witches. And in the following description
of the burning of the notorious poisoner, Madame Voisin, she
does show some concern for the agony of the victim, even if
her tone seems distressingly light to us:

> She appeared in the cart, dressed in white—appar-
> ently what one wears if one must be burnt. . . .
> My son asked a judge the other day if it wasn't a
> strange thing to fry a woman over a slow fire. "Ah,
> but there are mollifications," his friend replied, "be-
> cause of the weakness of the sex." "You mean they
> strangle her?" "No, but they throw logs at her head,
> or tear her head off with iron pincers." So you see,
> dear child, it's all not so terrible as one might sup-
> pose.

There was nothing she could do about the criminal justice
system, but she *could* have had an impact on the way families
put away their less attractive daughters into convents in order
to swell the dowries of the more marriageable ones, and it is
hard to suppress a start of indignation at the way she con-
dones her daughter's treatment of her oldest granddaughter.
Perhaps poor little Marie-Blanche de Grignan had a true voca-
tion, but I cannot but see something grisly in her grandmother's determinedly cheerful view of a cloistered life that she
would have loathed herself. Counseling that Marie-Blanche
be sent to an abbey where at least a Grignan aunt was abbess,
she comments:

> One can come home for a visit; one can go to the
> seashore; after all, one is the "niece of Madame."

She was, I suppose, making the best of a bad matter.
Where would she have got had she rocked the boat? "There
are things one must leave to providence," she would say; "all I

can do is write admirable letters that will have only the effect that it pleases God to allow them."

If she saw the atrocities, she saw also the glories of the reign. There were not only the splendid palaces, the music, the dazzling court; there was a great literature. Madame de Sévigné loved all that was finest in her time: La Fontaine, Molière, Racine, Bossuet, Corneille, but like a true member of the age she preferred Corneille to all. "Oh, yes, Racine is very fine," she writes the enthusiastic Françoise, "but nothing in any poet will ever even approach the greatest verses of Corneille," and she goes on to assure her daughter that she would have wept had she heard the grand old man reading *Pulchérie* aloud at the duc de La Rochefoucauld's. This tragedy, one of the last and weakest from the great poet's pen, deals with a middle-aged Byzantine empress who contracts a *mariage blanc* with an aged general who dotes on her. If one can understand how anyone could have wept at *that* experience, one may be as close as it is possible to be to the era. The glory of the Sun King could at times be rather garish.

But she felt that her era needed a sun king; that is the point. She was aware that his was an extraordinary reign and that great things were being produced in France, and she was determined that the crown and court should be worthy of all that was below them. She had a tendency, in other words, to "dress up" the establishment, to posit not only a monarch who deserved the eulogiums of his poets, but an army and a foreign policy that exemplified the Gallic concept of *gloire*. Thus in 1689 she could seriously write:

> We have no plan to attack anybody; we seek no battles or sieges; we are purely on the defensive, but in a manner so mighty as to cause our foes to tremble. Never before has a French monarch seen three hundred thousand men under his command. None

but the old Persian kings have had such a view. All
is new; all is miraculous.

So awe-inspiring is Louis that even the usually cool and
collected Madame de Grignan almost loses her head in an
interview:

> Is it really so that, in speaking with the king, you
> should have been drained of self-possession and
> stripped of all thoughts, conscious only, as you say,
> of his awesome presence?

Not only must the friends who suffered disgrace accept it
humbly; they must be bathed in gratitude if restored, even
quixotically, to favor. The Lord giveth and the Lord taketh
away. Here is how Madame de Sévigné describes the unexpected recall, after nineteen years of exile, of her friend the
marquis de Vardes, banished for his officious but hardly criminal attempt to warn the queen of the rising favor of La Vallière:

> The king, who considers and weighs everything si-
> lently in his head, suddenly announced one fine
> morning that Monsieur de Vardes would be back in
> court in two or three days' time.

Everyone was delighted; everyone applauded. And when
Vardes appeared in unfashionable clothes at which the king
snickered, Madame de Sévigné records admiringly that the
unfortunate man explained with tears in his eyes: "Ah, sire,
when one is wretched enough to be out of your presence, one
is not merely unhappy. One becomes ridiculous!"

Yet somehow these passages, taken in context, do not jar.
Madame de Sévigné is so honest, so sensible, so down-to-earth
in the description of her home life and her friends, so infinitely varied and witty, and possessed of such a wonderful
turn of phrase that we accept the pious references to the

political and military excrescences of Louis' theory of divine
monarchy as we might accept the half-perfunctory breast-
crossing or bead-telling of some devout old peasant woman.
And indeed there is a kind of woman's revenge on that world
of men and soldiers. By reducing it to a mere backdrop of the
more credible stage created by her letters, she somehow mas-
ters it, puts it in its place.

There is a wonderful passage in which she describes a per-
formance of *Esther* at St. Cyr in the winter of 1689. Here we
have a glimpse, so to speak, through a telescope at a slide
showing the basic elements of the glory of the reign: Versailles, Racine, Madame de Sévigné, and last and also least,
the Sun King himself:

> It is difficult to give any idea of what a delicious
> performance it was: it can never be imitated. It is a
> blend of music, verses, choruses and performers, so
> perfect, so complete, that one could wish for noth-
> ing more. The girls who play the kings and other
> characters seem made for the purpose. One is rapt;
> one cannot bear to have it over. It is all so innocent,
> so sublime, so touching, so faithful to religious his-
> tory.
>
> The king came up to us afterwards; he said to me:
> "Madame, I am sure you were satisfied." I replied
> composedly: "Sire, I was enchanted. It was beyond
> words." He continued: "Racine is very clever." I
> responded: "Sire, he is all of that. But truly, so are
> these young women. They play their parts as if they
> had never done anything else." He agreed. "How
> true!" And then he passed on, leaving me the object
> of universal envy.

It used to be commonly said that Madame de Sévigné lav-
ished too much of herself on a daughter who was unworthy of
her, that Madame de Grignan was a cold, selfish creature who

used her mother to pay her husband's debts and to advance his interests through friends at court. But twentieth century psychiatry has altered all that. The fact that Madame de Grignan probably wrote almost as voluminously as her mother could not be explained by mere self-interest, nor could a person as perceptive as her mother have been fooled over so many years into believing, as she states over and over, that she has the most loving child in history. Madame de Grignan may have had her unpleasant side. She could be hard and snobbish, we know. But her involvement with her mother was far from calculating. It was deep and emotional.

Madame de Sévigné could not have been an easy parent to live with. When she and Françoise were together, she was forever fussing over her, reminding her to take care of her precious health, to take this or that medicine, to put on this or that cloak or other garment. And then her too lavish praises of her child in front of others must have been at times embarrassing. "Are there really women like that?" Françoise's bored sister-in-law once retorted to her mother-in-law's endless encomiums of the divine Grignan. And finally, Madame de Sévigné outshone her daughter in company. It must have been frustrating to have one's mother always receiving the laughter and applause. One can understand that, even loving her mother as she did, she preferred living apart from her. It was a relationship that was easier to handle by correspondence than face to face.

Madame de Sévigné was often hurt by Françoise, but this was unreasonable of her. She should have seen that the molten lava of her maternal passion was sometimes scorching to its recipient. Her passion for her daughter dominates the long correspondence and seems to seethe over the borders of seventeenth century forms as the passion of Phèdre for her stepson overflows the classic structure of Racine's drama. But if it was a bit too much for Françoise, it supplies an added interest for us. It provides the letters with a unity they might otherwise lack, a contrast of extremity with moderation, of burst gates with strong walls, of unbridled emotion with contained common sense. Without it Madame de Sévigné might seem overly judicious, a touch too conventional, a little too "Louis XIV." We know that she is short-changing her poor son to help pay her son-in-law's debts; we don't approve, but we understand.

As Sainte-Beuve puts it, there are two styles among the major writers of the era: the uniform, academic "simplified with difficulty" style of the classicists and the free, capricious, mobile, untraditional style of all the others. Madame de Sévigné, of course, is among the latter. "She lets her pen trot, the reins, so to speak, resting on the neck of her steed; as she proceeds along the way, she strews it with a profusion of colors, comparisons, images, wit and sentiment that seems to escape from her in all directions. And thus she established herself, without the aim or even a suspicion of it, among the greatest writers of the language."

V
Port–Royal and
the Arnauld Sisters

At the convent of Port-Royal, when news was brought of the liberation, after five years in prison, of the saintly Abbé de Saint-Cyran, guilty only of having once offended the ego of Cardinal Richelieu, just deceased, Mère Agnès was in the parlor, but, not wishing, even on so great an occasion, to break the conventual rule of silence, she conveyed the good tidings to those present simply by unloosing her belt.

Saint-Cyran had been the beloved confessor to the sisters of the convent. That he should have fallen into such durance at the displeasure of a prince of the church was received by his communicants as a fact to be bravely faced. They knew their obligation to ecclesiastical authority; they knew, too, that there were limits to it. Mère Agnès' gesture was the silent expression not only of her approval of the release, but of her disapproval of the confinement. A cardinal was a man—a great man, perhaps, but he could still be wrong. Soul for soul, he was no better than an abbess, or the humblest novice.

Convents in France had been convenient places to dump dowerless girls of good family. Sometimes if there was one particularly beautiful daughter, her plainer sisters would be bundled into a religious establishment to swell her portion as bait for a bigger fish. But the cloister was not always as dreary a life as might be supposed. Some of the houses were comfortable, even luxurious, and discipline was often relaxed. But when the Arnauld sisters, Angélique and Agnès, were entered in Port-Royal as small girls, early in the century, a new era was already in the making. Having never been exposed to men except their fathers, brothers and priests, they were to develop an independence founded on the spiritual life alone. It was to give them a force and a power that would change convents all over France.

Port-Royal consisted of twin religious houses, a convent in Paris and a sort of ecclesiastical community at Port-Royal des Champs, in the valley of the Chevreuse, near Versailles. The latter was populated not only by nuns, but by novices, anchorites and pious scholars, the latter sometimes living in austere retreat, sometimes with their families. A few great ladies of the court, now become devout, occupied private *hôtels* in the vicinity. There was a complex of gardens, fish ponds, bakeries and storehouses, with a special school for the children.

Both institutions were dominated throughout the century by the Arnaulds, who came originally from the Auvergne to establish themselves as eminent lawyers and magistrates in Paris. But when they turned at last to religion, they did so with lasting passion and uniformity. Two daughters of the founding father, Angélique and Agnès, became abbesses of Port-Royal when only girls, and their widowed mother followed them to the convent as Sister Catherine of Sainte Félicité, bringing her four younger daughters. Two brothers and two nephews joined the lay residents, and six nieces in turn became nuns, making a total of seventeen Arnaulds to leave their mark on the institution.

The clan was early identified with Jansenism, a Calvinistic doctrine, but within the Catholic Church, which taught that man could not hope, either by his own efforts or by faith alone, to attain redemption from original sin. Salvation could come to him only by grace, and God granted grace as God saw fit. There was little that an individual soul could do to attract this near whimsical favor, but there seemed to be implicit in the doctrine the idea that if he lived apart from the world, concentrating altogether on the spirit, if he truly stripped his heart and mind of all concern with material things (pleasures of the mind being included with those of the flesh), he might, just might, persuade God that he was a worthy recipient of grace. I doubt, however, that even this was admitted by the more orthodox Jansenists. I suspect that to them a man was supposed to annihilate his ego to the extent of accepting his own damnation.

The doctrine was enunciated in *The Augustinus* by Jansenius, bishop of Ypres, and adopted by the Abbé de Saint-Cyran, confessor to the sisters of Port-Royal. Another early convert was the great theologian Antoine Arnauld, brother of Angélique and Agnès, who incorporated it in his treatise *The Frequent Communion.* The Jesuits, who read into the sober and discreet lives of the near mystics of the Jansenist persuasion an implied reproach that other orders handed out absolution with a frivolous facility, developed a hatred of the sect that became in some of these leaders almost pathological. Through the Jesuit confessor of Louis XIV, they played on the young king's horror of the smallest political deviation to persuade him that the Jansenists were a threat to his sacred concept of absolute unity under an absolute monarch. They also persuaded the pope to condemn five alleged Jansenist propositions and to require all suspected of the heresy to sign a *formulaire* repudiating it. It was this *formulaire,* and the refusal of the nuns at Port-Royal to sign it, that led to a half century of persecution and the ultimate destruction of the convent.

What most impresses a modern reader of Sainte-Beuve's monumental history of Port-Royal is the contrast between the gloom of the Jansenist doctrine and the purity and high serenity of the lives of those who espoused it. The concept of man condemned to eternal torment for an original sin that he did not commit, and wholly dependent for his reprieve on the pleasure of a deity who might be placated by man's total abandonment of all pleasures of mind and body, is a chilly one to those reared on the Sermon on the Mount. Yet it had no such effect on the Arnauld family or their disciples. It is difficult to imagine individuals of a greater simplicity or charity. The Sisters Angélique and Agnès in long lives devoted to the worship of God and the administration of his convents on earth seem to have succeeded in suppressing their egos without suppressing the color or vividness of their strong personalities.

Angélique was the first to dedicate herself to reform. Port-Royal had been a typical convent, a kind of lax girls' boarding school where great ladies could live only mildly separated from the world in the lap of ease. She knew that reform would have to be gradual and that it would come largely by example. She knew that she would have to offend her own parents by establishing a more rigid role of cloture. She won everyone, from her superiors to her family, by her patience and persistence and by her ability to drive herself beyond human limits in the work she undertook. She and Agnès bowed cheerfully even to the orders that sent them away for years at a time to other convents to initiate new works of reform.

Racine in his *Abrégé de l'histoire de Port-Royal,* has given us a beautiful description of the atmosphere created by the sisters:

> Never has a religious house been imbued with a holier atmosphere than Port-Royal. Its every outward aspect inspired the deepest piety; one marveled at the grave and moving chants that praised the Lord; the simplicity and immaculateness of the church; the meekness and discretion of the inmates; the silence of the parlors; the aversion of the sisters

to even the mildest gossip, their indifference to worldly matters and even to their own personal affairs, being truly concerned with nothing outside of God. Ah, how many subjects of edification were to be found there! What peace and calm; what charity! Work without stint; prayer without cease, each seeking the lowest and most humbling task; no loss of temper, no quirks of personality—all simple obedience to reasonable instruction.

Why should this community, so self-contained—even, it might be said, so self-absorbed—have attracted so vicious an opposition? I suppose it was because the example of so Christian a life made the rest of the church seem hollow and worldly. When Henri de Montherlant wrote his moving tragedy about the persecution, he inserted stage notes directing that the Jesuit inquisitors be dressed to suggest great gaudy insects. It seems appropriate. Surely never in history has a more unoffending minority been more relentlessly calumniated. When Monsieur de Péréfixe was told that Mère de Ligny refused to sign the *formulaire* he shrieked at her:

> "Shut up! You're a little bigot, stuck-up and stupid;
> you push in where you're totally ignorant. You're a
> saucy baggage, an idiot! You don't know what you're
> talking about. One has only to look at your dumb
> face to see what you are!"

Why would the sisters not sign the *formulaire?* It was a complicated matter. There was a question as to whether the pope had correctly defined the five propositions of Jansenius that he condemned. Renouncing an ill-defined proposition could be a tricky business. One might find oneself renouncing Saint Augustine on grace. The great point was that the sisters had such a horror of falsehood that they would submit to any penalty rather than risk it. Of course, the Jesuits and bishops screamed that they were ignorant women setting themselves up against learned males. But even if their bodies were subject to ouster from the convent, even if they could be denied the sacraments by arbitrary men, their souls were sexless and subject to salvation. One of the sisters in Montherlant's play cries to the priest who denies her the eucharist:

> Today is the day of man. Tomorrow is the day of God!

The church tried to dry up Port-Royal by sending away the novices and the lay residents. Without recruits the sisterhood was doomed to extinction. Antoine Arnauld went into exile. Mère Agnès was banished from the convent, and by the time she was allowed to return, it was virtually a prison. Mère Angélique, who died in 1661, was spared the worst, but she saw clearly enough what was going to happen. Even in the crisis of her final illness, she found the strength to dictate a long letter to the queen mother justifying her convent against the charges of heresy.

It is sad to relate that, this task completed, Mère Angélique should not have been able to face her own end in peace. But instead of the resignation that might have been expected of a person of her character, the poor woman found herself assailed by agonies of terror. As Sainte-Beuve put it: "It was singular that this holy woman, who in the more than fifty-five years since she had taken the veil had never lost an absolute control over herself, should have had to undergo so frightful an ordeal." She saw herself before God like a criminal on the scaffold awaiting execution. "Nothing," she cried out, "that I have ever imagined equals what I am now undergoing!"

Should it really surprise us? How could a true Jansenist not have feared damnation? What faith could this woman have placed in a deity who might have omitted to save countless souls as pure as her own? It is a sad example of how much greater the Jansenists were than their doctrine. A religion that brought so little consolation to a person of the caliber of Mère Angélique must be gravely wanting. But Antoine Arnauld did not take it so. Here is how he—the Jansenist *par excellence*—answered his niece about his sister's unhappy end:

> Nothing could be more afflicting than what you tell me about the poor mother. God must wish to test her to the very end in making her endure this terrible purgatory of the suffering of the soul. But his spirit has always operated very differently among the saintly: some, penetrated with his goodness and mercy, are filled with peace and sweetness at the end. Others, having a more vivid sense of his infinite holiness, cannot comprehend how sinful man can appear before so sublime a judge; they are seized with a paralyzing fear that robs them of all joy or consolation. The first of these states is what we naturally want for our loved ones, but the second is still something grander and holier, as it begins to approach what Christ chose, at least insofar as he could, for himself. It is the burden of the strongest natures, of those most firmly established in piety.

In the end the government found that it had not the patience to await the demise of Port-Royal through the deaths of its surviving occupants. The convent was seized, the sisters dispersed to other houses, and the buildings laid waste.

Nothing more vividly illustrates the curious homogeneity of France in the great reign than the attitude of Jean Racine toward the persecutors of his sect. He had been born a Jansenist, part of the Port-Royal community, and had, with considerable difficulty, broken away to establish himself in Paris as a playwright. Needless to say, to a good Jansenist the theater was nothing but devil's work, even when it produced a *Phèdre* or an *Andromaque*. At thirty-seven Racine, returning to his early piety, quit the theater for good (except for two biblical

plays written later at the command of Madame de Maintenon) and became a respectable married man, a devout church-
goer and historiographer to the king. Posterity has deplored
his decision, but there is no evidence that he ever regretted it
himself. The moving account that he wrote of the persecution
of Port-Royal, though not published in his lifetime, is ample
evidence of what the convent meant to him.

He admits frankly in the *Abrégé de l'histoire de Port-Royal*
the painful truth that the greatest of convents should have
been the victim of the greatest of monarchs, but he attributes
the tragedy entirely to the ill will of the Jesuits and to the fact
that no proper defenders of the nuns had access to the royal
ear. A modern reader immediately protests. Should a great
monarch not have instituted some sort of unbiased hearing?
Racine, however, like Madame de Sévigné insists on separat-
ing his sovereign from the more odious events of his reign. His
sympathy was capable of remarkable stretches. It could embrace the guilty passion of his heroine Phèdre, the ringing
honesty and absolute courage of the Arnaulds, and the worldly
ambition and bigotry of Louis XIV.

The Arnaulds did not believe that Racine was doing anything for his or anyone else's soul by polishing and repolishing
his peerless Alexandrines, but they had a style of their own,
the high style that may result from total immersion in the
waters of selflessness. Here is a letter from a niece of Angélique and Agnès, Mère Angélique de Saint-Jean, to the
duchesse de Luynes, who had sent her her misplaced condo-
lences over the disgrace of Mère Angélique's brother, the marquis de Pomponne, a secretary of state, in 1679:

> A person dead to the world should not expect the
> honor that you do me, madame, in offering me con-
> solation for a worldly disgrace. I am all the more
> obliged for your goodness in going beyond the pre-
> cept that bids us weep with those that weep, in that

your sympathy extends even to those who do not weep, since such disgraces as my brother's do not merit the tears of those who know that we should weep only for sinners and for the temptations that beset our loved ones to prefer this world to a heavenly one. I have worried about my brother ever since he has been subject to such temptations. He is not yet secure, but he may be on his way now; the hope must be my consolation. I should not be so bold as to write to you in this manner, madame, were I not assured that you wish me to speak the language of the seekers of God.

It was some time, no doubt, before the duchess again saw fit to thrust her worldly sympathies on an Arnauld! She could now bear witness to the stuff of which martyrs are made.

VI
The Mancinis
and the Montespan

Giulio Mazarini was the most successful man of his age. That the grandson of a Sicilian peddler should have risen to govern France, marry his nieces to royalty, and put together the greatest fortune, the most voluminous library and the finest art collection in Europe was nothing short of a miracle in a day of strong natural prejudices and rigid class lines. It was not unlike the rise of Benjamin Disraeli, two centuries later, to the leadership of the British Tories. Cardinal Mazarin, like Disraeli, was infinitely resourceful, tightly disciplined, constantly observant. He knew when to speak loud and when to speak low. He was both a soldier and a diplomat; he could be rough and bluff, but he could also cajole. I have always thought of him as a kind of Iago—without the evil purpose. He never seems to have blinked an eye in assuming the different and even contradictory roles that he had to play. Thus he could be both amusing and businesslike with Richelieu, whose early confidence was his first indispensable acquisition; flattering and romantic with Queen Mother Anne (whose actual husband he may have become, as he was only a cardinal, never a priest), and wise, kindly, avuncular with the young Louis XIV.

A protégé of the Colonna family, Mazarin had studied law in Rome. But he gave this up for the more rapid advance of military life, and became a captain in the army of the pope. His dashing appearance and insinuating manners qualified him for diplomatic missions, and in negotiations with the French he attracted the notice of the great Cardinal Richelieu, who had accompanied the army of Louis XIII into Italy. This acquaintance was renewed later in Paris where Mazarin had been named nuncio, and Richelieu, thoroughly convinced now of the legate's astute political abilities, induced him to leave the papal service for his own and obtained for him a cardinal's hat. When Richelieu died in 1642 he left Mazarin to Louis XIII as his successor, and the king, who survived his great minister for less than a year, passed the wily Italian on to his widow, Anne of Austria, who, infatuated, invested him with all her power as regent. To a jealous court it must have looked as if it had all been done with mirrors!

But if Mazarin was smooth and fawning with the great, he was very different with his seven nieces, daughters of his sisters, whom he summoned up from Italy to join him in the Louvre. The function of these girls would be to establish his family among the greatest of Europe, and they had to be strictly trained to the purpose. The uncle was absolute boss; none of them were ever to question that. It is not surprising that none of these high-spirited young women ever wasted much affection on him. "Thank God, he's gone!" Hortense exclaimed when she heard of his death. "Isn't it extraordinary that a man of that mark, after working all his life to elevate and enrich his family, should be regretted by none of them? But if you'd seen how he treated us! Never was a man so sweet in public and such a tyrant at home."

The daughters of the cardinal's sister, Mme. Martinozzi, Anne-Marie and Laure, were of a sober disposition and a respectable deportment. The first became princesse de Conti, wife of a prince of the blood and sister-in-law of the Grand Condé, and was renowned for her piety and good works. The second was the duchess of Modena, who governed her small principality wisely and well as regent for her infant son until his coming of age allowed her to retire to Rome.

A very different spirit, however, was manifested by the five daughters of Mazarin's sister, Mme. Mancini. Only one of these was considered respectable by the standards of the day, the duchesse de Mercoeur, and she died young. The other four caused the names of Mazarini-Mancini to ring through Europe and to become synonymous with a hilarious disregard of all order and form.

It is impossible not to feel some sympathy for them. Subjected in easygoing France to the iron discipline of an Italian uncle, sneered at as parvenues by the court at the Louvre, moved as pawns to fulfill the family's dynastic ambition and destined to princes who could be counted on to look down on them, these charming but very earthy young women made early resolutions to take their lives into their own hands. To whom, after all, did they owe any basic loyalty? To their parents? But these had given up their children to Mazarin. To France? It was only the country of their forced adoption. To the uncle who had enriched them? But he had done it for his own glory, and anyway, he had stolen the money. They must have concluded that they owed nothing to anyone but themselves, and resolved to use every weapon that their sex had to hand.

Two of them tried for the king. The young Louis XIV was not only the rising sun, he was as handsome as any man in his court. Uncle Giulio wanted a good match, did he? Well, they would give him more than he'd bargained for! First Olympe and then Marie went after the monarch. Ex-queen Christina of Sweden, who saw Olympe and Louis dancing together, remarked that two such fine physical specimens should certainly be joined in wedlock. The queen mother, Anne of Austria, was not amused. Olympe was promptly married off to an Italian branch of the Bourbons, the comte de Soissons, who proved a cheerful *mari complaisant* with respect to her numer-

ous love affairs, including one (now permissible) with the king.
But Marie offered a more dangerous threat. Louis actually
wanted to marry her. The cardinal, whose proposed peace
with Spain had to be cemented by the king's marriage to the
infanta Marie-Thérèse, banished Marie from court and lec-
tured Louis sternly and effectively on his royal duties.

One wonders if Mazarin did not do so with a pang of re-
gret. To have been uncle to the king! The queen mother is
supposed to have threatened him with civil war (him, her
lover!) if such a match were made, and one can well believe it.
To a Spanish Hapsburg, blood would always come first. Anyway, Mazarin was too great a realist to bite off more than he
could chew. Marie was sent to Rome to marry Prince Colonna, whose father's steward her grandfather Mazarini had
been. When Colonna was small enough to point this out to
his bride, Marie retorted, "I know nothing of that. But I do
know that of all my sisters I am the most poorly wed." After
the first nuptial night the prince announced publicly his surprise and gratification at finding her a virgin. Was something
wrong with Louis XIV?

The cardinal was disappointed in his nephews, only one of
whom survived early youth, and he, created duc de Nevers,
was content to while away his life as a mere poetaster. So he
decided to adopt an heir and make him duc de Mazarin,
marry him to a niece and bequeath him the bulk of his fortune. Unfortunately for his plan, he picked not only the
wrong man but the wrong niece. Armand de La Meilleraye
was a cousin of the late Cardinal Richelieu and had been in
love with Hortense Mancini since she had been a small girl,
but there his qualifications ended. He added to a morbidly
jealous and possessive nature a dangerous streak of insanity,
possibly the same that affected other cousins of Richelieu
(and, it was rumored, the great minister himself), and Hortense could not abide a husband who was always trying to lock
her up, far from the great world and its delights. As duchesse

de Mazarin she was forever escaping from her husband, and he forever trying by force to recapture her, to the scandalization and titillation of European society. At one point Hortense joined her sister Marie, who had left Colonna, in Rome, and both eluded their consorts' patrols by fleeing into France dressed as men. The duc de Mazarin consoled himself in a prudish fit by mutilating the glorious nude statues of her uncle's collection and scattering the greatest fortune of Europe to the winds in three hundred lawsuits.

Olympe, comtesse de Soissons, and the baby Mancini sister, Marianne, now duchesse de Bouillon (wed to a nephew of Turenne) felt that their sisters had gone too far and were disgracing them. Olympe called loudly for their chastisement. But the "virtuous" sisters in Paris were to fall even lower than the non-virtuous in the public esteem as a result of their involvement in the notorious affair of the poisons.

In 1679, pursuant to persistent Paris police reports about the growth of a murder syndicate trafficking in death by poison, a special tribunal called the Chambre Ardente was established to bring the culprits of the devilish practice to justice. Some hundred and fifty unfrocked priests, practicing witches, abortionists, purveyors of love philtres and poisons, were arrested. Some of the greatest names of the realm were involved: a marshal of France, any number of peers and peeresses, including Mesdames de Soissons and de Bouillon. Not all of these were would-be poisoners by any means. Some may have sought to have their love objects frozen in fidelity; others may have simply wanted their fortunes told. But it seemed as if the very fabric of the splendid century was eaten up with the microbes of superstition and lust. In the three years that the Chambre Ardente sat, thirty-six persons were burned alive, including the famous witch Madame Voisin; four were sent to the gallows; thirty-six banished; and thirty acquitted. Eighty-one were imprisoned for life.

But suddenly, in 1682, the court was suspended and its

records impounded. Word seems to have got around among the accused that the only way to stop the terrible process was to implicate the king's mistress, Madame de Montespan. Anyway, it worked. When Louis was presented with evidence that his favorite had dosed him with love potions, he balked at the idea of adding the destruction of his reputation to that of his digestion. As Frances Mossiker has put it: "His imposing image might dissolve to one titter of laughter were the news to get out that this cock of the international walk was crowing on a craw full of aphrodisiacs; hand-fed for years by his mistresses on a mash of blister beetles, cocks' combs and cocks' testicles."

Both Olympe and Marianne appeared before the Chambre Ardente. Both held their heads high and retorted impudently to the judges. They treated the whole matter as an impudent joke that could hardly concern such great ladies as themselves. But enough was reported about Olympe to induce her to flee to the Spanish Netherlands where she was denounced by howling mobs as a witch. The poor woman was to spend the rest of her long life in exile, passing through Spain where she was accused of poisoning the young queen Marie-Louise, niece of Louis XIV, and eventually joining her sister Hortense in London. The latter had a brief final triumph as mistress of Charles II. But little was left in the end of the Mazarin fortune, and less of the Mazarin reputation. The girls had taken the only revenge they knew of on their uncle and on life.

Though he did not live to see it, Mazarin was more fortunate in the next generation of his family. Laure Mancini's son, the duc de Vendôme, won brilliant victories in Spain, though he lost the battle of Ramillies in Flanders. Olympe's son, Prince Eugène of Savoy, was known as the second-greatest commander of the era. When Queen Anne insisted that he was the first, he retorted, "Then it is you, ma'am, who have made me so," referring to her cashiering of the duke of Marlborough. Anne-Marie Martinozzi's son François, prince de Conti, known as the Grand Conti, an able soldier, was elected king of Poland, though the election did not hold. And Laure Martinozzi's daughter, Mary Beatrice of Modena, became the queen consort of James II of England, of whom more hereafter.

It is interesting to note that all three of the above-mentioned great-nephews of the cardinal were homosexuals. I note also that one of Olympe's other sons, the chevalier de Soissons, was so much in love with his aunt, Hortense de Mazarin, as to kill a man in a duel over her, and that Laure Mancini's second son, Philippe de Vendôme, was enamored of his aunt, Marianne de Bouillon. The freedom of the "Mazarinettes," their frank emancipation from family rules and customs, seems to have created a certain sexual confusion in their male descendants.

* * *

The Mancinis were at a special disadvantage in being not only foreign, but so stupendously rich. Their fortunes made them the natural targets of princes; they started as victims, even if they later became victimizers. None of them achieved anything like the power and influence of such royal whores as the duchess of Portsmouth in London or the marquise de Montespan at Versailles. The last is the great mistress of the era. She had the career Hortense Mancini might have had, had she been born more French and less wealthy.

Saint-Simon, who was a cousin of Madame de Montespan, says (with rare generosity) that she only reluctantly gave in to the king's advances, and begged her husband to take her away from court, but this is believed by no one today. It seems perfectly clear now that she went after Louis deliberately, carefully stalking her prey. She had all the advantages of the Mancinis: wit, beauty and high spirits, but she was also of the highest French birth, a Rochechouart, daughter of the marquis de Mortemart, and had a natural imperiousness that would well fit the position of *maîtresse déclarée*. For Athénaïs de Montespan would never be content with the king's love, like the docile Louise de La Vallière. She aimed at being virtually queen.

In attaining her objective she treated everyone, including the little queen, with a high hand. Athénaïs was a person who could carry off arrogance; she could even make it attractive. She subjected the king to her tantrums; she spent his money like water; she was outrageously selfish, but she also had humor and verve and style. Somehow she had been missing in that most splendid of courts. The queen was a cipher; La Vallière had been a mouse. The Sun King needed a sun queen, and he knew it. He was proud of the way she dazzled the court and the ambassadors.

Their liaison lasted for fourteen years. The bastards of this double adultery were not only legitimated but married to princes and princesses of the blood. The marquis de Montespan even added to the drama of his wife's apotheosis by draping his carriage in mourning and surmounting its roof with stag's horns. If the Mancinis had defied their era, Athénaïs had done so and gotten away with it.

And yet even at her giddy peak she never totally lost her sense of humor or her basic horse sense. She could even be generous when it cost her nothing. This seems little enough, but in that hardened court it was something. Thus we have seen her being kind to la Grande Mademoiselle, even when she was robbing her. And when the king was carrying on a platonic love affair with the serene Madame de Maintenon, governess of his bastards, and a more fleshly one with Mlle. de Fontanges, Athénaïs had the coolness to quip to the former, "The king has three mistresses now. That slut Fontanges has the body; you, the heart; and I, the title!"

Of course, her star was declining. After the birth of her last child, the comte de Toulouse, according to Nancy Mitford:

She grew enormously fat, and in spite of two or three hours of massage every day, it was seen, when she got out of her coach, that each of her legs was the size of a thin man. She was always inclined to be blowsy; now she used too much scent, which the king hated. . . . Her temper had become truly appalling.

But her conversation was as good as ever. Here is how Saint-Simon describes it:

It is hard to imagine anyone more witty or more exquisitely urbane; in particular, she had a special turn of phrase and a gift for selecting the apt word that was all her own. It was enchanting to listen to her, for she had what was almost a special language, so that her nieces and the other ladies in her household took the habit of it, and even now one recognizes it in those few who are left. It became the natural way of speaking in the families of her brothers and sisters.

This was the "Mortemart wit" which Proust, a devoted Saint-Simonian, may have had in mind when, in *Le Côté de Guermantes,* he endowed the social circle of his duchess with the *esprit de Guermantes.* His samples of it are little gems of smartness and fatuity; they have the special, snobbish humor of a clique, appreciated more by its members than by outsiders. I have no doubt that the Mortemarts would have sounded less brilliant to us than to Saint-Simon.

The affair of the poisons is generally supposed to have marked the end of Athénaïs' favor and the high tide of Madame de Maintenon's, but in fact the king had begun to tire of his mistress' scenes and tantrums some time before. Younger women could take care of his lust, and the governess was a better companion for his now troubled soul. Did he suspect Athénaïs of poisoning the poor little Fontanges, who picked this time suddenly to die? If he did, it seems strange that he would allow her to live for several years more at court so close to him and to Madame de Maintenon, whom she now passionately loathed. Do *we* suspect her of murder? I think not. I can perfectly imagine her stretching herself out, nude, on an improvised altar and allowing the blood of a stillborn babe (or perhaps a murdered one—she wouldn't have had to know or ask) to be dripped on her stomach. But she never strikes me as a killer. To go back to Nancy Mitford, I can hear Athénaïs telling the Voisin, in her high, quavering voice, that she has time that day for only "one black mass."

Ultimately the king and Madame de Maintenon could not stand having her so close, and she was directed to leave the court. Saint-Simon has drawn one of his finest portraits of Athénaïs in retirement, determined to seek her salvation in penance and strict religious observance, but still "imperious, proud, domineering, scornful, with all the faults that perfect beauty and unlimited power bring in their train."

She kept an apartment at a convent in Paris, but she journeyed about restlessly, sometimes taking the cure at Bourbon, for she lived in a constant, morbid dread of death, sometimes visiting her sister the Abbess of Fontevrault, sometimes holding state in her great château of Oiron, whose rooms were filled with portraits and statues of the Sun King and where a great oaken bedstead behind a gilded railing topped by a crown futilely awaited the royal return. She slept with her own curtains undrawn, lest death should seize her behind them, and she kept servants in the room all night, talking, playing cards or eating so that they should not become drowsy.

She became an institution in her retirement, and all France came to call on her. She never lost her regal manner, and received her guests seated in an armchair, the only one in the room. People accepted the little game that she was playing.

She was, after all, a kind of *monument historique,* and she never lost her wit or charm. One can well imagine why it became "the thing" for parents to take their young to call on the great Madame de Montespan. At the end, which came suddenly at Bourbon, she lost her fear and thanked God in the presence of her household for permitting her to die far from children whose very existence was a reminder of her sin.

VII
Mary of Modena

Our progress now takes us across the Channel to England, but
via Italy, through a great-niece of Cardinal Mazarin. It will be
recalled that one of his Martinozzi nieces married the duke of
Modena, a member of the ancient family of Este, from which
union issued one son and one daughter, Mary Beatrice. The
existence of the latter, at the age of fifteen, was brought to the
attention of James, duke of York, as providing a possible successor to his recently deceased wife, Anne Hyde. The duke
was twenty-five years older than the intended bride, but that,
of course, made no difference to anybody. He was the heir
presumptive of his brother, Charles II, whose marriage had
been issueless; he had only two daughters and needed a son,
and being a Catholic, he wanted a Catholic bride. It was
characteristic of James that he should have blandly brushed
aside the angry protests of his largely Protestant nation.

But not only did the English protest; the bride did. Mary
Beatrice had never even heard of England, and she was determined to be a nun. Unfortunately for her, the earl of Peter-
borough, dispatched to inspect, found her fascinating. He reported:

> She was tall and admirably shaped; her complexion
> was of the last degree of fairness, her hair black as

jet; so were her eyebrows and her eyes, but the latter so full of light and sweetness as they did dazzle and charm, too. There seemed given unto them by nature sovereign power: power to kill and power to save; and there were all the features, all the beauty, and all that could be great and charming in any human creature.

According to Agnes Strickland, the conscientious but emotional early Victorian scribe of the queens of England, Mary Beatrice (who became her particular heroine) had an unexpected ally in the pope, Clement X, who, because of territorial disputes between Modena and the papal states, refused to sanction a match that might bring to the Estes the powerful support of England. But Miss Strickland seems not to have been aware of this letter from the pope to Mary Beatrice in 1673:

Dear daughter in Christ, since the design of the duke of York to contract alliance with your nobility reached our ears, we return thanks to the father of mercies who, knowing our solicitude for his glory, is preparing for us in the kingdom of England an ample harvest of joy. Considering, in effect, the influence of your virtues, we easily conceive a firm hope that an end might come to persecution still smoldering in that kingdom and that the orthodox faith, reinstated by you in a place of honor, might recover the splendor and security of former days, an effect which no exterior power could accomplish and which might become due to the victory of your piety, the inheritance of your eminently religious family. You can therefore easily understand, dear daughter in Christ, the anxiety which filled us when we were informed of your repugnance for marriage. For although we understood that it arose from a desire, most laudable in itself, to embrace religious discipline, reflecting that in the present occasion it opposes itself to the progress of religion, we were nevertheless sincerely grieved. We therefore, fulfilling the duties of our charge, earnestly exhort you by these presents to place before your eyes the great profit which may accrue to the Catholic faith in the above named kingdom through your marriage.

It may well have been this appeal to the poor girl's sense of duty that caused her to withdraw all opposition to her elevation. From now on, and indeed until her death forty-five years later, she was to have one sacred mission in life: to bring her new people back to the old faith. Mary Beatrice was a woman of medieval traditions. She believed more in kings than in their kingdoms. Her loyalty would be to the House of Stuart, wherever it happened to be—in England or in exile—so long as it remained Catholic. She had quite as much force of character and ability as any woman considered in this book, but it was her fate to work for the past and for medieval ideas. It is surprising that the Roman church of her day did not see fit to beatify her.

She started her English career a bit awkwardly, but one must remember her youth and inexperience. When her mother, who had accompanied her to London, returned to Italy, she found herself, a mere girl, in a strange land, wed to a husband old enough to be her father, and detested by most of the population as a Catholic. Small wonder that she proved herself a bit gauche. In Edinburgh she picked the wrong time to be prickly about her rank, refusing to sit down with the famous Scot general, Dalziel, who retorted brusquely that when he had dined with the emperor, the duke of Modena, her father, an imperial vassal, had served them at table. And when the young Frances Villiers died, Mary Beatrice had the indiscretion to relate a dream in which the poor Protestant girl cried out to her that she was burning in hell and reached out a hand that was too hot for Mary Beatrice to touch. It may be imagined how well this went down in the court of Charles II! But worst of all was the fury that Mary Beatrice exhibited when her husband continued his old habit of sleeping with homely mistresses (his brother quipped that he must do it as a penance); she brought priests in to harangue him, and threatened to retire to a convent.

Time and hardship, however, were to act as stern preceptors to the new duchess. The unpopularity of the Yorks necessitated their removal, on different occasions, abroad, to Scotland and Holland. The Commons was constantly threatening to cut James out of the succession. And actual prosecution seemed possible during the time that Titus Oates, a seventeenth-century Joe McCarthy, was accusing everyone of treason, and when Mary Beatrice's secretary, Taylor, was tried and actually hanged for having received moneys from the French embassy to be disbursed among members of Parliament to further Gallic and Roman Catholic interests. His distressed mistress announced his fate to her brother in Mantua, saying, "Certainly the state of all Catholics in this country moves one to pity, and what is worse, some poor miserable beings, constrained by necessity, are abandoning our holy faith."

When Mary Beatrice finally assessed the full strength of the odds arrayed against her, she began to assume some of the heroic stature with which Agnes Strickland credits her. At some point she seems to have accepted the unfaithful nature of her husband, and treated her early fits of jealousy as faults. James Stuart's character is a difficult one for us to assess. Certainly he was a courageous and capable naval officer; he conducted himself in a royal manner and he was careful and conscientious about public moneys. Historians differ about his treatment of prisoners and rebels, depending on the extent to which they believed him aware of the atrocities committed by

Judge Jeffries in the suppression of the rebellion against him
as king by his brother's bastard, the duke of Monmouth. But
it seems clear that he countenanced ancient tortures during
his visits to Scotland, and certainly it was incumbent on him
to know what his judges were doing. His greatest fault was his
stubbornness; once he became a Catholic convert, he set himself blindly in the path to bring England back to the faith.

When Charles II died in 1685, slaughtered by his doctors
—their prescriptions, it has been said, would have been fatal
to a young, healthy man—the long-badgered Yorks must have
seemed to see the gates of heaven opening for England at last.
The prospect was temporarily blurred by the brief rebellion of
Charles's bastard, the charming duke of Monmouth, but this
attempted usurpation was soon crushed, with hideous reprisals, and poor Monmouth, after groveling in vain at his uncle's
feet, was led off to a sadly botched decapitation. The new
King James II and Queen Mary Beatrice could now be
splendidly crowned, and their long-delayed plans for the re-
conversion of England to the ancient faith, so happily fore-
seen by Clement X at the time of their engagement, imple-
mented.

Did James really plan to reestablish the old religion by force
if necessary? There is some evidence that Mary Beatrice at
least favored a course of persuasion and that she feared the
influence on her husband's stubbornly orthodox nature of the
Jesuit extremist Father Petre. And it has always been argued
by James's defenders, notably Hilaire Belloc, that he was really only seeking toleration for Catholics, that his true goal
was freedom of religion throughout his realm. It is also true
that the seven bishops who were sent to the Tower of London, precipitating the rebellion in 1688, were incarcerated
because they refused to read from their pulpits James's edict
of toleration. But the fact that his issuance of such an edict
was itself an unconstitutional act, added to his filling of government and army posts with Catholics, gave Protestants in

that violent age grave reason to suppose that he might not hesitate to use the forcible measures of his first cousin and longtime protector Louis XIV, once he should feel it safe for him to do so. Perhaps he would not have. We shall never know. That he trusted other people so implicitly—even his own Protestant daughters, Mary and Anne, although warned against them by reliable French intelligence—may have indicated that he was himself trustworthy. But then again he might have been vulnerable to the argument that he could save his own and his wife's souls only by a rigorous reestablishment of the Roman church.

The Protestants in England were willing to put up with James II so long as Mary Beatrice did not produce a male child, and when, after fifteen years of marriage and a couple of stillborn sons, she had produced only one surviving daughter, people began to breathe more easily. Mary, now married to William of Orange, would be queen, and after her Anne, and after her, Anne's little son, the duke of Gloucester, all securely Protestant. But when in 1688 Mary Beatrice gave birth at last to a healthy male child, later to be known as the Old Pretender, the exasperation that ensued led to the revolution that replaced James II with his daughter Mary and her husband, William of Orange. The cruelest part of the whole business, cheerfully joined in by both James's daughters, to whom Mary Beatrice (only a few years older than they) had never shown anything but kindness, was the so-called "bedchamber plot," the fabrication and spreading of a widely accepted rumor that the queen had not been pregnant at all and that a strange baby had been smuggled into her chamber in a warming pan.

Mary Beatrice, at her husband's express command, fled to France with her infant son, escorted by Lauzun, whom we have met with la Grande Mademoiselle, where she was established in considerable state in the château of St. Germain. When King James followed her into exile, the always ceremo-

nious Louis XIV insisted on bringing his cousin personally to
Mary Beatrice and witnessing their tearful reunion.

"Madame," he said, "I bring you a gentleman of your acquaintance, whom you will be very glad to see." Mary Beatrice uttered a cry of joy and melted into tears, and James
astonished the French courtiers by clasping her to his bosom
with passionate demonstrations of affection before everybody.
"The King of England," observed a witness, "closely embraced the queen his spouse in the presence of the whole
world!"

Mary Beatrice must have been a very charming woman.
Her warm greeting of her poor old banished unfaithful husband is certainly lovable. And almost everyone but her stepdaughter Anne succumbed to her appeal. Earl Godolphin, the
great lord of the treasury, was supposed to have been in love
with her. Madame de Sévigné was instantly won to her, seeing
her at Versailles dressed to perfection in black velvet "with a
most majestic air." And even the duke and duchess of Marlborough, who had been primary aides to William of Orange
in the uprising that dethroned James II, owed their own wedding to Mary Beatrice. Poor and relatively obscure, the young
John Churchill and Sarah Jennings might have had to wait
much longer had she not taken them under her wing and
sponsored their union. Much thanks she got for it! Mary Beatrice may have reflected bitterly that it was like the hypocriti-
cal English to dub a revolution "glorious" in which two
daughters had driven their old father from his throne.

But for all her loveliness she had the toughness of a fanatic.
James survived his deposition for only thirteen years, but
Mary Beatrice survived it for thirty, and in all that time she
was the real spirit of the little court at St. Germain. She made
herself an expert in all matters of etiquette and palace politics;
she was vital to the task of extracting money and troops from
Louis XIV. And this she had to do with the help of a motley
group of Catholic peers, lovers of lost causes, soldiers of for-

tune, adventurers and malcontents. It was not much, but it
was quite enough to cause constant anxiety to London, to
raise expectations, to plan assassinations, to bring about
bloody reprisals. What did the cost in life mean to Mary
Beatrice? No sacrifice was too great if directed to the restoration of the old faith and the old monarchy. It was God's will,
after all, not hers.

When James died in 1701 at St. Germain, on the threshold
of the great War of the Spanish Succession, Louis XIV, pre-
cipitated into disaster by his sense of kinship with the expiring
monarch and their long joint reverence for the divine right of
kings, decided to recognize his son as king of England. Had
he not done so, William III, as William of Orange was now
styled, might have failed to drag England into the war. The
bereaved Mary Beatrice extolled the Sun King in a kind of
Nunc Dimittis:

> It was a miraculous interposition, in which, with a
> heart penetrated with a grateful sense of his good-
> ness to us, I recognize the hand of the Most High,
> who was pleased to raise up for us a protector in his
> own good time, by disposing the heart of the great-
> est of kings to take compassion on the widow and
> orphans of a king whom it pleased God to cover
> with affliction here below.

And she wrote in this high tone to her stepdaughter, the
princess Anne:

> I think myself indispensably obliged to defer no
> longer the acquainting you with a message, which
> the best of men, as well as the best of fathers, has
> left with me for you. Some few days before his
> death he bid me find means to let you know that he
> forgave you from the bottom of his heart, and
> prayed God to do so too; that he gave you his last

> blessing, and prayed to God to convert your heart,
> and confirm you in the resolution of repairing to his
> son the wrong done to himself.

It was perhaps characteristic of the myopia and arrogance of the little Stuart court that its heralds on the balconies of St. Germain should have, following the tradition laid down by Edward III three centuries before, proclaimed James III king, not only of England, Scotland and Ireland, but of France! One would have thought that might have convinced the Sun King that he was harboring an adder in his bosom.

The years of Mary Beatrice's widowhood were mostly sad. Although she had time and energy to give to the sacred cause, she spent as many of her days as she could spare in the Convent of Chaillot. Tragedy followed on tragedy. The lovely princess Louisa, her mother's consolation and the brightest light of the little court at St. Germain, died of smallpox, and one of the Allies' conditions in the Treaty of Utrecht was that Louisa's brother James, the Old Pretender, leave France. Mary Beatrice herself suffered long and painfully from a cancer of the breast and expired at St. Germain in 1718.

"The queen of England," wrote the duc de Saint-Simon, "died after ten or twelve days' illness. Her life, since she had been in France, had been one continual course of sorrow and misfortune, which she sustained heroically to the last. She supported her mind by devotional exercises, faith in God, prayer and good works, living in the practice of every virtue that constitutes true holiness. Her death was as holy as her life."

To which one can only comment that she might have been a good queen had she lived two centuries earlier.

VIII
Mary II

When Bishop Burnet instructed Princess Mary of Orange, wife of the stadtholder of Holland and daughter of James II of England, about her rights of succession to her father's throne, she expressed astonishment to learn that if she became queen, it would be as sole sovereign and that her beloved William would be, in England anyway, a mere consort. She declared at once that she would never reign without him as cosovereign, and the English rebels, who proposed to oust her Catholic father and substitute Mary for her infant half brother to guarantee a Protestant rule, found her absolutely intractable on this point. The conditions (obviously dictated by her husband) that they had ultimately to meet were (a) that William should reign with her as cosovereign, (b) that the rule should be his and not hers, and (c) that Mary's sister Anne's succession, in default of issue of William and Mary, should be postponed until the death of whichever of them survived the other. All that Anne's supporters were able to obtain was that the younger sister should take precedence over any issue of William by a *subsequent* marriage.

The woman who thus obediently turned over all of her power to her husband was willing to subject more than herself to him. She did not hesitate to prefer him to every other inherited loyalty or interest of her life. Not only were her father, her father's infant son and her sister Anne swept out of William's way; the resources and manpower of her native land were rallied to support William's lifelong struggle against Louis XIV. And all this without a qualm!

She is certainly the most disappointing woman, *qua* woman, considered in this essay. And what is most extraordinary about her connubial submissiveness is that she was in no way a mouse. On the contrary, she was bright, gay, witty and could be very funny. She loved to dress up and go to dances or to racy comedies. She accumulated vast closets full of clothes. Nobody meeting Mary and Anne when they were girls would have anticipated that, as queens regnant of England, the brilliant older one would be a mere consort, and the plain, dull younger an active power in world affairs; that Mary would devote her reign to helping her husband embroil her country in a costly war and that Anne would get England out of it.

Mary Stuart was born in 1662, just two years after the restoration of her uncle, Charles II, and it did not seem likely then that she would ever wear his crown. He had just married and was expected to have children; indeed, he had already sired several bastards. And Mary's own parents were still raising a family and might have a son. Furthermore, her father, the duke of York, later James II, was in bad political odor as a Roman Catholic, and there was always the danger that Parliament might seek to exclude him from the succession. It was true that Charles II had required that his nieces be brought up as Protestants, but even so, once Parliament should take it into its head to regulate the succession there was no telling where it might stop. An additional inducement to bypass the York family might be found in the fact that Mary's mother, Anne Hyde, was a commoner, the daughter of a lawyer (though a most distinguished one; he became lord chancellor and earl of Clarendon), and James, who while duke of York had seduced and impregnated her under promise of marriage, had only reluctantly made good his word at the express command of his brother.

The first duchess of York, for all this, was a great lady and had a royal manner. She couldn't resist chocolate and grew round as a ball, but she had wit and presence and must have been very good company, despite her fretting at her husband's constant infidelities. She would very likely have made an excellent queen, far better than the usual German princess always available in the royal marriage market, but she died young, in 1671, when her daughters Mary and Anne were only nine and six. The girls grew up in a cloistered, female environment where love had to be pretty much supplied by fantasy. It is not surprising that both of them formed early passionate attachments to other girls and poured their hearts out in a romantic correspondence that to modern eyes suggests a good deal more than was probably in it.

Mary became something of a beauty, tall and high-spirited, with a flair for dress. By the time she had achieved the marital age of fifteen, the now established sterility of her uncle's marriage had placed her closer to the throne, although her father's recent match with an Italian princess, Mary of Modena, only a little older than herself, still made any succession by daughters unlikely. Charles wisely decided that Mary's marriage had better counterbalance the increasing Catholicism of his brother's domestic circle. The second duchess of York was a devout Roman, and it would be hardly feasible even for the king to provide that *her* children be raised as Protestants. It was decided that Mary should wed Charles's nephew, the young Dutch stadtholder, William of Orange, son of the late princess royal of England and next in line, after Mary and Anne, to its throne.

The fact that he was a dozen years older than Mary, a couple of inches shorter and a solemn, humorless man, totally preoccupied with Dutch politics, made no matter. A princess' tastes in those days were never consulted. Mary, in storms of tears, bewailed her impending exile in vain to her aunt. "But I had to leave Portugal when I married your uncle," Queen Catherine told her. "Yes, but you came to England!" was the bitter retort. The only objection to the match was that it might give a black eye to Charles's magnificent first cousin and personal ally, Louis XIV. The latter saw, more clearly than anyone else on the international scene, that the dour little stadtholder was already the principal opponent to his ideas of Gallic expansion. To the historian Macaulay, William's resistance to France was the chief glory of the sovereign whom he considered England's greatest; to Agnes Strickland it was simply the result of William's pique at having been offered one of the Sun King's bastards as a bride. To this writer, William's impassioned crusade against French hegemony started as a patriotic resistance to aggression and grew at last into something more like an obsession.

Louis XIV *did* object to the match; he told the duke of York: "You have given your daughter to my mortal enemy," and cut off Charles's latest subsidy. But Charles had no intention of being in the French king's pocket; it did not hurt to show one's independence on occasion. At the ceremony, when the groom, to symbolize his endowment of the bride with all his worldly goods, placed a handful of gold and silver coins on the open bible, the jovial king bade Mary put them in her pocket, for it "was all clear gain." And indeed those coins were to represent the sole deposit by the Dutch in English coffers to pay for the millions of pounds and thousands of corpses that English involvement in their struggle would cost. But no one then dreamed that so minor a prince would ever wield so great a power, and the courtiers must have smirked when Charles, escorting the couple to the bedchamber, encouraged the awkward groom with the bluff words: "Hey, nephew, to your work! Hey, St. George for England!"

For all this heartiness, the marriage was not to be blessed with issue, though it turned out to be far happier than anyone could have predicted. This seems to have been entirely Mary's doing. William was not only as jealous and autocratic a husband as might have been feared; he was unfaithful to her with both sexes. He had a long affair with Elizabeth Villiers, one of the maids of honor who accompanied Mary to Holland, and, in later years, with the handsome young Arnold van Keppel, whom he made earl of Albemarle. According to the French ambassador, William always kept Mary down, making her stay indoors with nothing to do but read and embroider, surrounding her with Dutch women and sneering at her English relations, even including their common grandfather, the "martyred" Charles I. He allowed her no pleasures that were not his own and begrudged her the practice of the Church of England, going so far as once to kick her communion table. By all reports he dominated her completely.

Yet Mary seemed to love it. She never appeared crushed, or played Griselda in such a way as to bring odium upon her disagreeable spouse. On the contrary, she continued to show high spirits. Unlike William's mother, who had held herself too high for the Dutch ladies, she became a true Hollander and made herself popular in society. She even dared in time to oppose William, though only in minor female matters where opposition was traditionally accepted, such as indulging her taste for gypsy fortunetellers or spicy theatricals. She was the perfect spouse for the egocentric male, a slave who looked like a slave only to him.

Politically, Mary was equally docile. She fell in with all of William's plans even when they involved betraying her own kin. When the duke of Monmouth, handsome bastard of Charles II, came to Holland, it was evident to everyone that he was looking for support in his bid for the throne on the death of his father, hoping that an illegitimate son might be preferred to a Catholic brother. Charles II, a loving father but a strict legitimist, had no idea of disinheriting his brother James, and it was made perfectly clear to all that Monmouth's ambitions were not to be countenanced by any of the royal family. William, however, unwilling to give up any card that might be profitably played in his own still secret bid for the English crown, instructed Mary to be agreeable to her cousin, and she spiritedly flirted with him. After the death of King Charles and the execution of the rebellious Monmouth by James II, Mary maintained a loving correspondence with her father and stepmother throughout their short reign, so that her own enthusiastic part in the English revolution in 1688, which transferred their throne to her and William, came as a complete shock to them. And when the princess of Orange, now Queen Mary II, arrived at Whitehall Palace in London, she ran through the state rooms examining her loot with an unfeigned delight and satisfaction that shocked even an observer as hard-boiled as Sarah Churchill. One wonders if Mary was even chagrined by the retort of an ex-mistress of her father, whom she snubbed: "Remember, ma'am, if I broke one of the commandments *with* your father, you have broken another *against* him!"

As queen, Mary was forced, even against her will, to exercise the ruling power when William III, in his long absences to Ireland and the Netherlands, left her as regent. But except for one or two appointments to her adored Church of England of which he might not have strictly approved, she regarded herself totally as his agent and interpreter. Yet she acted with such authority and efficiency that one cannot help but wonder if, had she succeeded to the throne like Elizabeth I, unmarried, she might not have been a great queen.

How did William accomplish it? How did he manage to turn this intelligent, lively woman, to whom he was neither kind nor faithful, into so effective a robot? Was she brainwashed? Was she ridden with guilt at having produced no heir for him? I think not. I suggest that if one carefully considers how the problems of the world may have appeared to her as a girl, one may find a clue to the answer she was seeking.

She and Anne were widely decried in their day as unfilial. They were considered worse than Goneril and Regan, for King Lear's daughters had at least not hounded him from a throne that he had resigned of his own volition. But how did James II look to Mary? From earliest childhood, at the insistence of her uncle, Charles II, who always deplored his brother's dangerous public espousal of a faith that he himself secretly shared, she had been brought up a Protestant and taught to believe that Catholicism was deeply inimical to the welfare of England and prejudicial to her father's own succession to the throne. Then James had compounded his error by marrying a young papist and producing a son who would be reared as a Catholic and take the throne ahead of Mary herself. What was her duty to such a man? Her contemporaries premised it on the filial relationship alone. All a man had to be was a father, and his children, *ipso facto*, owed him a duty. But Mary perhaps did not see it that way. She may not have understood why she owed any duty of allegiance to a man who had married her seduced mother only under orders from the crown and whose goal in life was to bring England back to a faith that she deemed a false one. And insofar as a personal relationship was concerned, James had almost surely shown her the parental casualness of the era, and he had certainly been continually unfaithful not only to Mary's mother but to the young stepmother of whom she had become fond.

What was England to Mary when she left it at fifteen? A nation that had cut off her grandfather's head and might well do the same to her father's. What was her family but her stolid sister Anne, and a stepmother misguidedly devout? What were her English friends but Elizabeth Villiers, who proceeded to become William's mistress? It seems perfectly possible that William may have struck Mary as the only man with the strength necessary to cope with the crazy world in which she had been raised. He was not a stubborn bigot like her father or an impractical saint like her grandfather, and he

did not laugh at everything like Uncle Charles. The world was
a serious matter, and perhaps only a man as serious and as
single-minded and humorless as William could hope to cope
with it. Anyway, what alternative did she have?

There might even have been a sexual attraction in the very
coldness of William's nature, so unlike that of the volatile
Stuarts who seemed to have made such a mess of things. All
except Uncle Charles, and weren't his compromises a bit
much? Having all those mistresses and taking money from
Louis XIV? Mary, without allies, in a strange country, had the
alternative of a haughty and self-pitying isolation, like her late
mother-in-law, or of making the best of her situation by win-
ning over the man who had been given, after all, an absolute
power over her. The best way to do that was to fall in love
with him and to stay in love. Somehow she managed it.

Mary died in 1694 of smallpox, at the age of only thirty-
two, after a reign of six years. Her exiled father, living on the
charity of Louis XIV at St. Germain, declined to go into
mourning, as did his little shadow court. William continued
to reign alone until his death in 1702, the only English sovereign to have a woman, his sister-in-law to boot, as his heir
apparent. He had absented himself as much from England as
he possibly could. In constant ill health, it must have been
agony to him at the end to know that he would not live to
witness the final humiliation of his great enemy, France. But
the ultimate struggle was clearly on its way. Mary had been
well used.

Because the War of the Spanish Succession (1701–13) was
the culmination of the imperialist thrust of France and the
resistance of Europe so central to the lives of the women
studied in this book a few words should be said of it here.

For years monarchs and statesmen had been brooding over
the devolution of the Spanish empire upon the death of the
childless, chronically ill, half-lunatic Spanish king, Carlos II.

One of the two principal contenders was the Dauphin, son of Louis XIV, whose mother had been a half sister of Carlos. She had renounced her rights of succession in Spain on becoming queen of France, but it was a legal question whether this had not been nullified by the nonpayment of her dowry. To avoid a union of the French and Spanish crowns, the Dauphin had been willing to assign his right to his second son, Philippe, duc d'Anjou. The other claimant was the archduke Charles, brother of the Holy Roman Emperor, whose grandmother, an aunt of Carlos, had never renounced her Spanish rights.

France, England, Holland and the Holy Roman Empire, like the expectant heirs of a quixotic millionaire who seek to ensure themselves against a cut-off, drew up a partition treaty by which they purported to dispose of a Spanish empire that belonged to none of them. Nothing could have been more galling to the moribund Carlos. When he learned that it was proposed that the archduke Charles should have Spain, the Indies and the Spanish Netherlands, while Anjou should receive Naples, Sicily and Milan, he executed a will, as a final gesture of protest, bequeathing all his domains to Anjou, and then expired. Louis XIV seized advantage of the technicality that one signature (the emperor's) was missing to the treaty to brush it aside and accept the testament. Presenting his grandson to the court at Versailles, he introduced him as Philip V, King of Spain.

He might have got away with it, to the despair of William III, had he not proceeded to commit an act of the grossest arrogance and folly. When the exiled James II died at St. Germain, Louis recognized his son publicly as king of England. It was all that William needed. On the last day of the year 1701 he went in person to open Parliament and solemnly reminded the new Whig majority of their responsibilities. "The eyes of all Europe are upon this Parliament; all matters are at a standstill till your resolutions are known. If you do in good earnest wish to see England hold the balance of Europe, and to be indeed at the head of the Protestant interest, it will appear by your right improving the present opportunity."

The speech was an immense success; it circulated through Europe like a speech of Winston Churchill in World War II. William bequeathed to his unfortunate, peace-loving sister-in-law Anne the War of the Spanish Succession, which would last almost all of her reign. By an ironic twist he also bequeathed to her the one general who might have won it, John Churchill, the man he would not use in his own lifetime to do the job that he could not do himself and that he wanted, of all things, to see done.

William's great posthumous war was the goal of his life and consequently of Mary's. It might almost be said that the vast conflict put in motion by one sister had to be ended by the other. The war involved all of Europe and both Americas; it was fought in Flanders, Germany, Italy, Spain and Canada, and on the Mediterranean and the Atlantic. One side was made up of the "Grand Alliance": England, Holland, Portugal, Denmark and the Holy Roman Empire, with a host of German principalities. The other was the "twin crowns," France and the Spanish Empire, with aid from Bavaria and Cologne. The perfidious duke of Savoy, despite one daughter on the Spanish throne and another married to the oldest son of the Dauphin, shifted sides throughout the conflict.

What was it all about? The most commonly given reason is that of William III: the need of the Grand Alliance to protect itself from the growing power of France, now made even more threatening by the presence of a grandson of Louis XIV on the throne in Madrid. But might not the other candidate, the archduke Charles, brother and probable successor to the emperor, have reconstituted the German-Spanish world empire of Charles V? The archduke was, in fact, actually elected to succeed the emperor; Philip V never succeeded Louis XIV. And what about the greed of England and Holland for trade routes and monopolies? Why did an England that feared only France have to seize and keep Gibraltar?

It seems odd in retrospect that so many Englishmen should have been so keen about prosecuting this war. Couldn't they see that Spain was nothing, that its vast domains were held together, so to speak, by string? That even if Philip V retained his throne, he was bound to develop (as indeed he ultimately did) a pro-Spanish, even an anti-French bias? Couldn't they foresee that the archduke Charles would be elected, as the Hapsburg heirs had for centuries, to the imperial crown? Couldn't they suspect that the people who had the greatest reason to fear the military aggrandizement of the Sun King, namely the Dutch, had taken full advantage of the rule of William III to embroil the English in an essentially Dutch problem?

But we in America need not feel superior. We have only to remember Vietnam.

IX
The Duchess
of Marlborough

If Mary II was the most disappointing woman of the era, Sarah Jennings was certainly the most exasperating. The wicked fairy godmother who had not been asked to her christening must have sent the one gift that would make all the others ultimately futile: the stubborn, lifelong conviction that she, Sarah, was always in the right and everyone else in the wrong. Against this her beauty, her brilliance, her courage, her honesty, even her patriotism, were to count for little. And Sarah was not only resolutely determined to show the world it was an ass, she expected to be complimented on her perspicacity.

She was born to one of those families that, without any particular claim to rank or fortune, somehow managed to attach themselves like barnacles to courts and to be on intimate terms with royalty. Seventeenth-century palaces, after all, were too vast to be filled entirely with great nobles, and princes were too grand to distinguish between the lesser grades. They took what was there, particularly when what was there was as handsome and lively as Sarah Jennings. In the court of the duke of York in the 1670s it is hardly surprising that the princess Anne—slow, unimaginative, already on the dumpy side—should have been dazzled by Sarah, five years her senior and the inamorata of John Churchill, the handsomest officer in London, who was even supposed to have fathered the last child of Charles II's mistress, Barbara Villiers! Poor Anne must have lived vicariously in Sarah's romance. Who would not have given up even royal birth to be such a Venus adored by such a Mars?

Sarah did not find it in the least head-turning that a dashing officer and a Stuart princess should both be in love with her. The fact that John obviously needed money and court influence to get ahead and that Sarah had only a modest dowry and was the child of an eccentric old woman vaguely associated with witchcraft, was no deterrent to a girl who knew how to play her trump cards of beauty and wit. John soon found himself totally in love with her, and he was to remain so for life. He did not, it seems, at first have marriage in mind, but Sarah had all (and more) of the will power needed to keep him firmly in check until they had been formally united. When this had been accomplished, she was able to devote her attention to her other admirer, take charge of the princess' life and household, and make them instruments in the promotion of the Churchills' career.

The marriage of Anne to an amiable nonentity, Prince George of Denmark, a union in which John Churchill's brother may have played a role, removed the danger of a counterinfluence in royal favor, and the princess, pleased with her affectionate and connubial husband and delighted with the regular companionship of her brilliant friend, was always on the lookout for ways to serve the latter. During the English Revolution in 1688, Sarah and John, never keen for lost causes, joined the prince of Orange and helped to turn Anne from her father to her sister. Sarah even recognized that it would be necessary to subjugate Anne's right of succession to that of Mary's husband William in order to unite the factions. After all, it was better for Anne to be next in line to a couple that had been childless for a decade than to have a father and a young brother ahead of Mary and herself. And what was good for Anne was bound to be good for Sarah and John.

So when Sarah was only twenty-eight it looked as if the brilliant future for which she had planned so carefully was assured. But then came disaster. John, who always liked to hedge his bets, had maintained a secret correspondence with the exiled court of James II at St. Germain (of which Sarah's sister, the duchess of Tyrconnell, was a member), and this was discovered by the agents of William III. The wrath of the king generated an answering resentment in Sarah. She inflamed Anne against her brother-in-law the king, whose high-handed treatment of poor George of Denmark had already caused great bitterness, and the two women henceforth referred to the monarch as "Caliban." There were plenty of people to report this to William's adoring wife, who at once ordered Anne to dismiss Sarah from her service.

Anne and Mary were always a hopeless combination. The former was slow and silent; the latter quick, tense, vivacious. And Mary resented the fact that her younger sister should have a faithful husband and a son who might succeed the divine William. Sarah probably seemed to be the easiest way to get back at her.

Sarah should probably have bowed to the royal mandate; her sway would have been just as strong at a slight distance. But she did not think so. If she left the princess for two weeks, she wrote to a friend, her influence would be gone forever. Ingratitude was certainly a well-known characteristic of royalty in general and of the Stuarts in particular, but Anne seems to have been an exception to the rule. There is evidence that she deeply resented the waiver of her succession rights to William so strongly urged by the Churchills (she complained that there had been less ceremony in her release of her interest in three kingdoms than in the conveyance of a cottage), but she seems never to have thrown this in Sarah's face. Indeed, as we shall see, she showed almost superhuman patience with her importunate friend.

Sarah, anyway, remained with Anne, and together they defied the queen. When the latter evicted them from the Cockpit, an adjunct of Whitehall, they moved to Syon House, offered to Anne by the duke of Somerset. And Sarah even had the nerve to appear in court with her mistress before the outraged sovereign!

The star of the Churchills seemed definitely on the wane. John was actually sent to the Tower on a treason charge, and though soon released, he was deprived of his military assignments. But all this was reversed in 1694 by the totally unanticipated death of the young queen. William could not afford to be on bad terms with an heir apparent whose genealogical claim to the throne was superior to his own, and the breach with Anne was grudgingly made up. John Churchill was not restored to his military command—William was always too jealous of him for that—but he was made governor of Anne's small son, the duke of Gloucester, and Sarah continued to rule the rehabilitated princess. When William died, only six years after his wife, and Anne became queen at last, the courtiers might have exclaimed of Sarah, as Banquo did of Macbeth:

"Thou has it now: king, Cawdor, Glamis, all!"

She was groom of the stole, keeper of the privy purse, the all-powerful favorite of the new sovereign. John, soon made duke of Marlborough, was captain-general of the Allied forces against France. The campaign in Flanders that he boldly extended to the Rhine would in the next year culminate in an overwhelming victory at Blenheim. And the Churchill prizes were not only political and military, they were financial. John's command contained perquisites that enabled him to lay the basis with apparent legality (though this has been strenuously questioned) to an immense fortune. It certainly looked as if the Marlboroughs were now beyond the reach of

any opponents. And so they were. No one could have toppled
them but themselves. It took Sarah a long time to accomplish
this, but where there's a will, there is apt to be a way.

To comprehend what happened, one must examine Sarah's
relationships with the two persons who were the sources of
her power: her husband and the queen.

Marlborough's personality has always been a difficult one to
make out. Every observer agreed that he had great looks and
charm. His most remarkable characteristic seems to have been
his equanimity: he preserved his patience and good manners
in the very heat of battle. He never, so far as one can make
out, lost his nerve. War to him was a science, perhaps even a
magnificent and complicated game. There is no trace in his
record of any animus against the enemy. On the contrary, he
maintained what to modern eyes would seem an almost treasonable correspondence with the Stuart court at St. Germain
and with his Stuart nephew, the duke of Berwick (bastard son
of the exiled James II and Arabella Churchill), one of the
great generals of the French. But in a day when commanders
made war by the book, conforming to the dictates of the
season and weather and sending polite messages across the
lines to their opponents (though abandoning the poor local
populations to loot and rapine), Marlborough, while just as
polite as his politest contemporary, made war with only one
object: to annihilate the other side. It was he who did what
William III could never have done: persuade the seven prov-
inces of Holland to risk their forces under his command outside their own soil in a daring march into the heart of Bavaria
to send the armies of the Sun King reeling back to France.

Jonathan Swift, no friend of Marlborough, who indeed was
part of the faction that eventually caused his dismissal, recognized the peculiar nature of his military genius, seeing him as
a new factor in war that might, like the atomic bomb of a
later era, ultimately prove as dangerous to his own nation as to
the enemy. Marlborough might have been "covetous as hell

and ambitious as the prince of it," but, as Swift eventually asked, had any "wise state" ever set aside a general who had been consistently successful for nine years and whom the enemy dreaded? Indeed, as Louis XIV was to put it when he heard of Marlborough's ultimate removal: "This will do all for us that we need." Has any commanding officer ever received higher tribute?

Macaulay in his history of Britain makes Marlborough out to be a great villain, but Winston Churchill has corrected (perhaps even overcorrected) the record. Every writer, including the subject's distinguished descendant, concedes that Marlborough was close in money matters, and one can shake one's head or not at his accepting money as a young man from the duchess of Portsmouth, whose favors he shared with King Charles, but I think few would agree with Macaulay's venomous appraisal that "in the bloom of his youth, he loved lucre more than wine or women." As Winston Churchill retorted, "He loved Sarah more than all."

John Churchill married Sarah Jennings despite her lack of the dowry that he so sorely needed and in the teeth of parental opposition, and the only person who ever suspected him of infidelity in all the years of their marriage was his unreasonably jealous wife. The deep note of love sounded in his early letters, which in the last year of her life his aged widow sought to burn as too personal, but noted in a hand quavering with age that she "could not doe it," characterized his correspondence with her to the end. To quote his descendant once again:

> Neither the heat of battle, nor the long drawn anxieties of conspiracy, neither the unsanctioned responsibilities of the march to the Danube, nor the tortuous secret negotiations with the Jacobite court ever disturbed the poise of that calm, reasonable, resolute mind. But in this love story we see him

panic-stricken. The terror that he and Sarah might miss one another . . . overpowered him.

His love was fully returned, but Sarah was not concerned with his comfort or ease as he was with hers. She took his passion, characteristically, simply as her just due. But if she was unwilling to pay for it with any restraint of temper, she still valued it to the full, as she nobly expressed in her old age in the famous letter rejecting the proposal of the duke of Somerset:

> If I were young and handsome as I was, instead of old and faded as I am, and you could lay the empire of the world at my feet, you should never share the heart and hand that once belonged to John, duke of Marlborough.

Yet this same woman chose the moment of Marlborough's departure for the Blenheim campaign to make a fearful scene of jealousy that sent him off sad and wretched. And she totally ignored his warnings from the front that it was the sheerest folly for her to choose to be a passionate Whig when her sovereign was an equally passionate Tory. The secret of her power over him was that he dreaded her scenes. The man who never flinched in the bloodiest battles shrank before a ranting woman. But it was love that made him do so, not weakness, except to the extent that love is weakness. The only thing in the world that frightened him was her unhappiness. Perhaps he feared for her sanity.

But Sarah at least loved him. Unfortunately, she did not even like the queen. John's and Sarah's scenes might end in bed, but there was no end to those that Sarah made at Windsor, at Kensington, at Hampton Court. She had a low opinion of poor Anne, both as a woman and as a sovereign. It must have been highly frustrating for a woman as socially capable as Sarah, who could easily imagine herself presiding over the very greatest court, to watch the queen boring her guests at receptions by talking about the weather and holding a fan over her mouth. One can almost believe the story that Sarah, having put on the queen's gloves by mistake, tore them off and flung them to the floor in a gesture of personal revulsion.

Sarah had no conception of self-discipline, and she gave her impatience with Anne and her dull court full rein. Her absences began long before Anne's accession, dating back to the death of Sarah's mother in 1693. They increased steadily as Sarah's children occupied more and more of her time while poor Anne was losing one after another of her own ill-fated progeny. And then Sarah began to be interested in the classics, a taste that the unread sovereign could certainly not share. The duchess seemed to have forgotten or deliberately ignored her own warning to herself that a fortnight's separation would be fatal to her sway.

The rise to power and influence of Abigail Hill, the poor relative whom Sarah unwisely promoted to be Anne's bedchamber woman, will be told in the next chapter. Suffice it to say here that what really brought about Sarah's dismissal from her court offices was not so much Abigail's replacing her in the queen's affections as Sarah's discovery of this. And this discovery did not occur until 1707, many years after the fact!

So great, indeed, had been Sarah's dominion over Anne that the latter had taken every possible precaution to conceal from her the inroads made by Abigail in the royal affections. Furthermore, the queen had no wish to substitute one tyrant for another. Abigail was to find promotions yielded only grudgingly, even when her status as a favorite had been accepted. What the queen wanted was an intimate, a gossip, a back-rubber, a hand-holder. This was why, when Abigail married, Anne attended the wedding in secret. She did not dare tell Sarah.

Even when Sarah finally discovered what was going on, she

could have preserved her positions, and probably even much of her influence, had she been able to accept Abigail. After all, the bedchamber woman was giving Anne only what Sarah had neglected to give her. But Sarah's rudeness became more and more shocking. By 1706 she no longer hesitated to throw the errors of Anne's unfortunate royal forebears in her face. Would not any rational person have expected the daughter of a dethroned monarch and the granddaughter of a decapitated one to resent this warning?

> I desire you would reflect whether you have never heard that the greatest misfortune that ever happened to any of your family has not been occasioned by having ill advices and an obstinacy in their tempers.

And finally, in 1708, Sarah went to the ultimate extreme. She taxed the queen openly with a lesbian attachment for her bedchamber woman:

> . . . I remember you said at the same time of all things in this world you valued most your reputation, which I confess surprised me very much, that your majesty should so soon mention that word after having discovered so great a passion for such a woman, for sure there can be no great reputation in a thing so strange and unaccountable, to say no more of it, nor can I think the having no inclination for any but of one's own sex is enough to maintain such a character as I wish may still be yours.

Poor Anne put up with that treatment as long as she could, but Sarah was incapable of the smallest compromise. What she did in the end was to present the queen with the choice of Abigail or herself. She virtually forced Anne to take Abigail. Sarah's dismissal from all her posts was followed in less than a year by her husband's. The duke and duchess went abroad, having no wish to remain at home while a triumphant Tory government, led by Abigail's cousin Robert Harley, patched up the peace with France that the duke had planned to dictate at Versailles. The Marlboroughs were rich and famous, but they would not again affect the policies of Britain.

It is difficult to think of any person in history who threw away as much as Sarah threw away. Some observers have wondered if she was not partially insane. Others have attributed her intemperance to hysterial grief at the death of her oldest son and to the strains of a difficult menopause. But have we not all known persons like Sarah? For whom nothing is ever right and who greet the greatest good fortune with a blow in the face? Marcel Proust understood such characters, creating one in Madame de Gallardon, who was always willing to sacrifice her greatest social ambition to the immediate satisfaction of making a disagreeable remark.

Sarah has had her admirers. A person so outspoken, so honest, so direct, will always command a following—after she is dead. But I must confess that I find it almost unbearable to follow the train of her self-destruction. In the end, when John was gone and she had antagonized her two surviving daughters, she was left alone except for a group of grown-up grandchildren who minded their manners with an eye to her last will and testament.

Her relentless fight to make the government honor Anne's pledges to complete the colossal mass of Blenheim Palace, which must have loomed bigger and bigger and more and more expensive as the victory that it commemorated retreated into the past, gave her ample occupation for her later years. She did not even like the edifice, and her husband, who had loved it, was dead, but that was no reason to let the British treasury off the hook. Of course, she fought with the great architect, Sir John Vanbrugh, an artist who had the rare capacity to rear mammoth residences free of the least vulgarity, but here she was dealing with a clever writer as well as an inspired builder, and he had the last word. In his final letter to her he compares his own dismissal, in favor of what he disdainfully describes as a "glassmaker," with the Tories' dismissal of Marlborough and the consequent waste of his victories:

> I shall in the meantime have only this concern on *his* account [Marlborough's], for whom I shall ever retain the greatest veneration, that your Grace, having like the queen thought fit to get rid of a faithful servant, the Tories will have the pleasure to see your glassmaker, Moore, make just such an end of the duke's building as her minister Harley did of his victories for which it was erected.

But let us take our leave of poor Sarah at a greater moment, say at the peak of her fame and fortune. It is an August night in 1704, and the queen is playing dominoes with Prince George in the bow window of the long gallery overlooking the terrace at Windsor. An officer, Colonel Parke, dusty and exhausted, hurries in bearing a penciled note scribbled on the back of a tavern bill. It is from the duke in a Bavarian village called Blenheim, and it must be delivered to the duchess alone. Sarah glances through it quickly and then turns to read it aloud, in ringing tones, to the royal couple:

> "I have not time to say more but to beg you will give my duty to the queen, and let her know her army has had a glorious victory!"

X
Lady Masham

Winston Churchill, in his life of his great ancestor the first duke of Marlborough, has two devastating comments to make about Abigail Hill. She was the smallest person, he says, who ever consciously attempted to decide, and in fact decided, the history of Europe, and she saved France as effectively, if not as gloriously, as Joan of Arc. Yet Abigail's record in history seems as slight as Churchill's estimate of her character. Even her single likeness, the one in the National Portrait Gallery, has been questioned. She creeps in and out of the hall of great events by a back door, her face averted, her step quick and soft, her voice reduced to a whisper. It is as if she were actually afraid to attract our notice.

The duchess of Marlborough tells us that Abigail was one of four children of a bankrupt uncle of hers whom she rescued from a menial position in the household of a Lady Rivers. Abigail lived for some time with Sarah, presumably earning her keep by domestic labor, until 1697, when Sarah elevated her to the place of bedchamber woman for princess Anne. This was not a position for a woman of quality; it seems to have been more that of a lady's maid. Why was Sarah so trusting as to place Abigail so close to the about-to-be sovereign? Undoubtedly because it never crossed her mind that a creature so humble, so plain and so mousy, could ever replace her in the royal affections.

We have a partial list of Abigail's duties in the palace. It was her task to place the basin and the ewer before the queen for the royal hand-washing and to pour the water out of the ewer over her mistress' hands. She pulled on the queen's gloves when the queen was unable to do so herself; she brought the queen's chocolate and presented it kneeling. But her position was always inferior to that of a *lady* of the bedchamber. Abigail was basically a domestic servant; she could not touch the sovereign in a public ceremonial. For example, when the queen dressed, Abigail handed the shift and the fan to the lady of the bedchamber who assisted the monarch. The bedchamber woman's ministrations could be personal only in private.

But Sarah, of course, had unwittingly handed Abigail precisely the little gold key that would open the door to power. Anne, as we have seen, was the very opposite of her then dearest friend, the duchess; whereas the latter loved spacious halls and ringing declarations, the queen preferred the intimacy of small stuffy chambers and private confidences. She retreated in her palaces to little suites where the court could not follow her and where she could unbosom herself to a sympathetic few. Sarah could not conceive that anyone could be happier on a chaise-longue than on a throne. But the quiet, competent creature who knew how to soak Anne's gouty limbs in hot water and rub her aching back, who did not pester her with political questions or harangue her about distant battles, who was deferential and humble, yet at the same time perceptively kind, indeed almost loving, who understood how much even monarchs needed soothing and consolation, and who had the happy inspiration to call her "Aunt"—*this* was the friend that majesty required.

It is astonishing that even a person as unimaginative as Sarah should have taken so long to find out what was going on. It was not until 1707, according to her own account, that she discovered Abigail's intimacy with the queen. She learned then not only that her cousin had been secretly married, but that Anne had actually sponsored the match and attended the wedding.

Abigail's husband was Samuel Masham, a groom of the bedchamber of prince George and a courtier since his debut as a page boy. Sarah has described him for the ages as a "soft, good-natured, insignificant man, always making low bows to everybody and ready to skip to open a door." That the wife of the first soldier of Europe should lose out to the wife of such a toady speaks worlds for the value of flattery. Jonathan Swift, purchasing a supposed Titian for two pounds five shillings, reflects in his journal that if it turns out a fake, he can always pawn it off on Masham. But the poor fellow was still a good match for a lady's maid, even a queen's lady's maid, and there is no reason to suppose that Abigail was not happy with a husband who probably did pretty much as he was told and who certainly kept her constantly pregnant. He could, too, in time be made a peer, though the queen would need a lot of persuasion for this, fearing as she did that Abigail as a baroness might be too grand to continue her chamber duties. Needless to say, this fear proved groundless.

Sarah has vividly told the story of her disillusionment. When she upbraided Abigail for keeping her marriage secret and accused her of ingratitude and disloyalty to her patroness, this chit of a cousin behaved with aggravating meekness, protested that some malicious person must have slandered her to the duchess, reaffirmed her loyalty and devotion to her former mistress, and then—hardest of all for Sarah to endure—actually had the gall to assure her, perhaps with one of her lowest curtseys, that the queen would always be kind to her!

Sarah could rage and storm, sweep out of the palace, traduce Abigail to the queen, even insinuate that she had flared the true nature of the latter's dark passion for her chambermaid, but all of this only tightened Abigail's grip on the affections of the outraged monarch. Lying down after one of these scenes to have her aching back rubbed by her devoted companion, Anne must have sighed with relief that the terrible duchess had gone.

But if Sarah had been blind, others had not been. Dozens of sharper eyes were fixed daily on the sovereign, exploring new methods of approaching her. If Abigail had found an aperture, Abigail herself became one. Robert Harley, former Tory leader in the House of Commons, who was determined to break the Whig hold on the administration, must have blessed his lucky stars when he recalled that his mother had been a sister of Abigail's grandmother. What had once been a connection too low to be thought of had now become the finest twig on the family tree.

What sort of person did Harley have to work upon? The details are few. But it seems clear that Abigail was plain; her red nose was later a constant target of Whig lampoons. Jonathan Swift goes so far as to state that her looks had the advantage of preventing gossip about the nature of her long private sessions with Harley. In personality she seems to have been subdued, at least until she began to feel surer of her position. Sarah describes her own shock when, calling upon the queen by a secret passage and chatting with her alone, they were suddenly interrupted by Abigail, breezing into the chamber with the boldest and gayest air possible. As soon as she saw the duchess she pulled herself up, assumed an air of subservience, dropped an exaggerated curtsey and asked the queen, in the voice of a menial, if her majesty had rung. But the first impression was to remain indelibly in Sarah's mind.

One might suppose that as Abigail rose in prominence and came to be more closely observed, her personality would emerge from the mist of the bedchamber. But it is not so. To as shrewd an observer as Swift she was "a person of a plain sound understanding, of great truth and sincerity, without the least mixture of falsehood or disguise; of an honest boldness and courage superior to her sex, firm and disinterested in her friendship, and full of love, duty and veneration for the queen, her mistress." Yet to Lord Dartmouth she was "exceeding mean and vulgar in her manner, of a very unequal temper, childishly exceptious and passionate."

We know that Abigail liked cards, ombre and piquet, and that she played Purcell on the harpsichord to Anne's probably not undiscriminating ear. She cared passionately for her children, which was not a thing to be taken for granted in that day, and worried herself into a near frenzy when they were ill. She was a skilled mimic and could dress finely if the occasion called for it. Anne found her something of an enchantress, but it is difficult for us to tell why. Certainly, when Abigail ultimately turned against Harley, he seemed to mind it more than just for reasons of state. She evidently had a way of attaching the affections of her few intimates.

Turning now to the man who made such astute political use of her, we are faced with a character only recently salvaged from a bad press. Harley has long suffered from a reputation for deviousness, dishonesty and trickery, even in a political era when to be a trimmer was deemed no great disgrace. But Elizabeth Hamilton has done valuable research to establish the probability that it was Harley's passion for moderation and compromise that ultimately caused him to fall between the two schools of Tory and Whig, and to be excoriated by both. The mild, round, kindly face of his portraits, containing some of the innocuous fatuity of those of Samuel Richardson, seems to go more with what we know of the amiable, convivial, bibulous bibliophile who never lost his temper and never even seemed upset than it does with the man who, according to William Cowper, was born under a necessity of being a knave.

Harley had been a successful speaker of the House of Commons, a position calling for talents of settlement, and a Tory secretary of state ousted by Whigs who found him lukewarm, if not actually treacherous, in supporting the war. Sarah had early suspected him; her husband at last threatened resignation if he was not removed. Harley, with his habitual equanimity and good temper, had gone quietly into apparent retirement where he could plot not only his return to power but the return of moderation and reason to a world rent by stormy emotions.

Throughout the years 1708 and 1709 he made a habit of calling on his cousin Abigail and of corresponding with her in code. His letters must have offered a pleasant contrast to the anonymous, hysterical epistles that she was receiving from Sarah, warning her how the Greeks and Romans had disposed of base creatures who proved a menace to the state!

This was the period of the terrible battles of Oudenarde and Malplaquet—victories to be sure, but victories at a hideous price, acutely distressing to the queen—and of Marlborough's injudicious request to be made captain-general for life, which many interpreted as a bid for dictatorship. It was also the time when Louis XIV was offered terms of peace insulting to any proud monarch: he was requested to join the Allies in chasing his grandson from the Spanish throne. To Harley and Abigail, huddled in secret session in one of the overheated royal suites, it must have looked as if the Whigs were determined, by driving the French to desperation, to continue the senseless slaughter indefinitely.

At the end of 1710 Anne at length asserted herself. She dismissed Godolphin as lord treasurer and dissolved Parliament. A Tory victory was followed by the appointment of Harley as lord treasurer and the dismissal of Marlborough, and the way was cleared for overtures for a separate peace between Britain and France.

It is always tempting to suppose that the apparent wielders of power are mere puppets in the hands of those who subtly manipulate them. Anne must have been controlled first by

Sarah, then by Abigail. And Abigail must have been controlled by Harley. And who was Harley controlled by? Swift, whom he used as a political writer? Why not? But of course it is always possible that Anne made up her own mind, or that Anne agreed with Abigail only because Abigail agreed with *her.*

Abigail was known to have Jacobite sympathies, as did the queen herself. It might have been that, far from being the low, intriguing creature so many writers have supposed, she simply wanted to encourage the queen to put an end to the hideous carnage of the war and bring to England an era of prosperous peace by having the now childless Anne proclaim as her successor, not a German prince hostile to the Bourbons in France and Spain, but the son of James II, her own half brother James, the Old Pretender, who would unite the destinies of Britain with the great Catholic civilization of Latin Europe. Perhaps Abigail had a first vision of the Entente Cordiale.

The trouble with such theorizing is that Abigail never offers the least support for it. She herself seems determined to remain obscure, even small. She has not left a line or a quote to indicate even a hint of political vision. The only time we see her actively pushing a promotion is for that of her unqualified brother, Jack Hill, who proceeded to make a mess of the Quebec expedition. She manages to elude any laurels that we would pin to her brow. And it seems likely that even her influence on the queen was exaggerated. She complained to Harley that it was very difficult for her to induce Anne to talk business and that she received constant rebuffs. He agreed that her influence was largely negative. "You cannot set anyone up," he wrote her, "but you can pull anyone down."

Yet despite the will of Sarah's biographers to make Abigail out a sly little sneak, she may still have been a decent enough person. She may simply have wanted to snatch what security she could for her rapidly growing family in a hostile court where fame might disappear overnight and poverty return. Sarah, of course, accused her of the basest ingratitude, but it must have been hard indeed to be the dependent of this terrifying older cousin, so handsome, so rich, so impossibly arrogant. One can sympathize with the dream (if dream it was) of the little seamstress, the plain bedchamber woman, the Cinderella, to pull down the mighty duchess and actually take her place.

Our only picture of Abigail in the days of her precarious glory—a picture that shows how desperately she had to toil to look after her family and stay in with the always unpredictable monarch—is made up of glimpses taken from Swift's *Journal to Stella*, that strange account of his life in London and Windsor that he periodically mailed to two lady friends in Ireland in the three years beginning in 1710. Swift, who in our day would have been known as a public relations officer, had come from Dublin to petition for greater crown benefits for the bishops of the Church of Ireland, but finding this too simple a matter for his brilliant talents, he had been taken on with a kind of retainer by the Tory leaders. It would be his job to persuade the public, or the Parliament, or the queen, of the desirability of their program for running the nation and ending the war.

Swift was obviously excellent company, and both the genial Harley and the charming, dissolute, brilliant and utterly undependable St. John loved good wine and good talk. The *Journal to Stella* has many references to the dinners in which these three met to discuss the world and its affairs, and in a matter of months Swift was able to make an entry to the effect that he was making his influence felt on the greatest ministers of the realm. Only the queen eluded him. She had hated *The Tale of a Tub* and was stubbornly averse to giving its author any court appointment. That Harley and his fellow minister, Henry St. John, should have carefully kept this from

Swift shows how deeply they valued the services of his powerful pen.

Abigail showed that she was capable of independence from
her mistress, at least where Swift was concerned, for she made
him one of her closest friends. Swift, who fully appreciated
her importance, had been watching her for some time before
they actually met. Observing that she is about to lie in, he
prays God to send her a healthy delivery, for her death would
be a terrible thing.

He is presented to Abigail on August 17, 1711, at a dinner
at Harley's, and he notes that she is used by all present with
mighty kindness and respect, as a favorite might look to. But
he also observes, in what is almost certainly not intended for a
compliment, that she is extremely like one Mrs. Malolly who
had been his landlady in Trim. Only ten days later Abigail
gives birth to a boy, who roars like a bull at his christening,
and from now on she appears regularly in the pages of the
journal.

Swift soon discovers her sharpest problem and what he
terms a great state secret: namely that the queen, keenly sensi-
tive of how much she has been governed by the late Whig
ministry, is resolute that it shall not happen again, so that she
looks with extreme jealousy and suspicion even on those who
delivered her from the hands of the Whigs. Abigail has to be
ever more assiduous, more persuasive; she can hardly spare a
day from the royal side, and if she does, the Tory leaders
scream at her. All this she must balance with the care of her
children and the safeguarding of her own fragile health. And
on top of everything she is always pregnant, the perennial
problem of pre-twentieth-century women.

Following the entries that refer to her discomfort makes
painful reading—though it would have been heady joy to
Sarah. After her lying-in Abigail suffers a bad cold and is lame
in one leg with a rheumatic pain. Yet the queen wants her for
cards and dancing. When she is at last able to return to

Windsor, Swift notes it is high time. The duchess of Somerset has taken advantage of the few days of her absence to make dangerous inroads on the queen's affections. Then comes the news of Jack Hill's disastrous campaign in Quebec. But Swift advises Abigail that she must attend a court concert to show that she is not cast down.

In December 1711 the terms of the proposed peace are debated in the lords, a majority of whom refuse to agree to any termination of hostilities while a grandson of Louis XIV still occupies the Spanish throne. This is a serious defeat for Harley, who has argued that the Spanish issue is not vital to British interests. Swift hurries to be the first to tell Abigail of the disaster. He taxes her fiercely with responsibility for it. Have she and the queen conspired to betray the peace party? The poor woman swears to the contrary. The queen has become inscrutable. It is impossible to tell whom she most favors. Had she not rejected the Tories the day before and given her hand to the Whig duke of Somerset to be led out of the hall? Swift in disgust quotes scripture to the effect that the hearts of kings are unsearchable. And he notes that in all of this turmoil Abigail still makes time to try on a petticoat!

In January Marlborough is relieved of his command, and Swift, sighing in relief, thanks providence that the queen has at last been persuaded to act in her own best interest. Abigail, despite the petticoat, has done her job, and she is rewarded, for Masham is made a peer. Swift comments on my lady's pleasure, noting that the peerage will be protection for her in the dubious future. He also observes that the new baroness at a court reception looks monstrous fine.

But misfortunes return soon enough. In March her son is very ill, and she is almost out of her mind with grief. By fall she is pregnant again and insists upon walking across a court-yard because of a fit of temper at her chairman, falls down, almost miscarries, but escapes with a black eye and a sore side. The next month she has a cruel cold, and early in 1713 she miscarries indeed. And then her son is ill again—she fears mortally—and she insists on staying at Kensington to nurse him even when the queen is at Windsor. Swift is outraged. It is clearly her bounden duty, both in the public interest and in her own, never to leave the queen, particularly with so many great questions still at stake. But when he tells her this, he complains that he may as well be talking to the wind!

And yet Abigail seems devoted to her stern mentor. When, soon afterward, it is determined (because of the queen's aversion to him) that Swift will be named dean, not of Saint Paul's in London, but of Saint Patrick's in distant Dublin, she weeps in her disappointment, and Swift notes that he has never been more moved to see such friendship. No more would they have their daily games of ombre and piquet in Abigail's hot, headache-making rooms. Did her stove account for the red nose? She would be reduced to mere memories of her brilliant friend as she plays the harpsichord, hour after hour, to the ever sickening queen.

The final years of Anne's reign were marked with unhappy dissension in the royal circle. Anne, increasingly ill, goutier and gloomier, was silent and impenetrable. Nobody knew anymore who was closest to her: Harley and St. John, frankly antagonistic now, struggled for Abigail's favor. The war was over but the succession was a hot issue. St. John had thrown in his lot with the Jacobites and was corresponding with the pretender. Harley was interested in the latter only so long as there was a chance that he might turn Protestant. He became a Hanoverian when convinced there was no hope of this.

It would be nice to suppose that Abigail switched her loyalties from Harley to St. John because she was faithful to James Stuart, but the record discloses the possibility of a baser motive. Was she nursing a grievance that he had not allowed her the profits that he had promised her from his South Sea scheme, whereby a company modeled on the East India should shoulder the national debt and use African slaves to build up trade from the western coast of South America? The reign was drawing to a close; Abigail had to feather her nest.

It seems that she was almost unbalanced now in her anxiety. Waspishly, she told poor Harley that he had never done the queen any service and was no longer capable of doing any. Swift found her too distraught to be of further use to anybody. Harley paid little attention to business, drank to excess and was disrespectful to the queen. Nobody trusted anybody.

When Anne died at last in 1714, Abigail was generally accused of caring only about what she could take away from the palace. But we must remember what a catastrophe the queen's death was for her. She had lived constantly at court for almost twenty years. She had no independent future, nor did Masham; they would have to live on the emoluments of their court career, modest indeed when contrasted with the loot of the Marlboroughs. The new sovereign from Hanover, George I, could hardly be expected to take care of a Jacobite, and Abigail, perhaps because of the very seclusion in which she had had to live with the queen, could have developed few if any powerful friends or protectors other than Harley and St. John, who were worse off than she. The former was to spend two years in the Tower; the latter to flee to the pretender's court. It was only natural that, for the sake of her husband and children, Abigail should make sure that she was in possession of all the things to which she was legally entitled—and maybe one or two more.

She retired with Masham to his family manor house in Essex where she lived until 1734. Nothing is known of her last two decades except that she was presented to queen Caroline in 1727. She had become a legend whom the latter had probably been curious to see. Masham? Mrs. Masham? Lady Masham? Was *she* still alive? Where had she been keeping herself all these years? Ah, but of course. She'd probably been hiding from the wrath of old Sarah Marlborough!

XI
Queen Anne

Alexander Pope, in a famous couplet from *The Rape of the Lock*, invokes Hampton Court:

Where thou, great Anna, whom three realms obey,
Did sometimes counsel take, and sometimes tea.

The lines provide a peculiarly fitting epitaph for a queen who managed to clothe her every activity in the same dull garb. Whether she listened to her ministers, or sipped tea, or ate enormous meals, or wrote long, self-pitying letters to her friends, or attended debates in the House of Lords, drawing the curtain of her box seat if the argument turned to the personality of the sovereign, or even when she followed the hunt, "like Jehu," in the phrase of Jonathan Swift, driving her big-wheeled chariot, especially made to encompass her vast round figure, she was always the same: a dull, grave, unimaginative woman whose strength seemed to be made up equally of reserve and stubbornness. She gave her name to an era brilliant for a literature that she never read, for battles of which she disapproved and for inventions that she did not understand. And yet she remains somehow an indispensable part of her glorious reign. She refuses to be reduced to a genealogical coincidence.

Agnes Strickland relates that the young princess, at her confirmation, drank three times from the cup of communion wine. It is not to be supposed that this represented an incipient alcoholism or even an undue thirst; Miss Strickland is careful to point out that Anne's tutor had been deficient in his instructions. But I nonetheless spy a characteristic of the woman in the gesture. Who else, tutored or untutored, would have thought to drink three gulps on such an occasion? There was a curious stubbornness about Anne that went with her lack of imagination and her intense self-absorption. What she happened to be doing at any one time she was likely to keep right on doing. This was the way she would handle Uncle Charles and his mistresses, her father, James, and his religious bigotry, her critical sister Mary and her impossible brother-in-law, William, the madness of civil war and even the high-handedness of her dearest friend, Sarah Churchill.

It seems likely that she spent most of her formative years feeling inferior. It was all very well to be the king's niece, but she was a long way from the crown, and it seemed that it might be her fate for life to be a minor princess in a brilliant, bewildering court—a dull, plain girl inclining to be stout, in a society of wit and beauty. Her mother died early, and her father, like most fathers of the era, particularly royal ones, paid scant attention to her. He and her young stepmother, whom Anne cordially disliked, were passionate devotees of a faith that Anne had been raised to believe was heresy. Perhaps partly as a defense, she clung to the Church of England which became one of the cornerstones on which she built her life. There is some of the essential Anne in the bland smugness and sublime assurance shown in this passage from an early letter to Mary:

> Our church teaches no doctine but what is just, holy
> and good, or what is profitable to salvation, and the

Church of England is without all doubt the only true church.

The only direction in which her emotions were free to fly was toward girls of her own age, and like her sister Mary she formed passionate friendships with such, putting herself fancifully in the passive role of an adoring husband, a curious prognostication of what her own docile spouse would be. When Sarah Jennings—five years older and in the full bloom of her beauty; bold, bright and stunning—came into her life, Anne was completely captivated. Was it possible that such a goddess could be interested in becoming her friend? If Anne could only be her slave! Which was precisely what Sarah was willing to allow her to become.

They were soon inseparable. To transcend the barriers of etiquette they played at being middle-class cronies. Sarah was "Mrs. Freeman," Anne, "Mrs. Morley." John Churchill was allowed to be "Mr. Freeman" and his friend Earl Godolphin was eventually included as "Mr. Montgomery." The Churchills were able to make a decent living out of the princess' household, and they may even have had a hand in her marriage to prince George of Denmark, an amiable dullard who would always do what he was told and was never going to rock anybody's boat.

George would never be to Anne what Sarah was to her; she would never sign herself to him with such effusions as "your poor, unfortunate faithful Morley, that loves you most tenderly and is, with the sincerest passion imaginable, yours." Still, she was devoted to him and bore him seventeen children, only one of whom, the little duke of Gloucester, outlived the nursery, and he not for long. When George himself died, after twenty years of conjugal obscurity, Anne mourned him sincerely, although Sarah, watching her friend continue as usual to consume her three huge daily meals, observed tartly that whereas grief was commonly supposed to take away appetite, in her mistress' case it seemed to do just the reverse.

Anne's ordeal as a mother is much noted in histories, but the full horror of it and its effect on her personality is less emphasized. In one week in 1686 she lost two children, Mary, a little over a year old, and Sophia, a few months, and she could hardly take out time to mourn them, so desperately was she nursing a sick husband. To have lost so much of one's time and vital energy in this fruitless effort to raise a posterity and to have to face the fact at the end of it all that the crown was still destined to a parcel of fertile and hated Hanoverians must have been a rough dose to swallow. Anne's defense against total despondency seems to have lain in a kind of willed lethargy, a determined interest in cards, in gossip, in court ritual, in things capable of being consumed, food and chocolates and syrups, in creating around herself a little world that did not reject or disturb her.

It is easy to see why Sarah made her ultimately fatal error of assuming that her friend could be led by the nose. For years Anne had taken the line of least resistance. Her role in the revolution that put her sister on the throne was confined to escaping from London with Sarah and pouring oil on the fiery rumor that her baby half brother, the prince of Wales, was a foundling brought into the palace in a warming pan. When Mary refused to accept the crown unless Anne agreed to place William ahead of her in the succession, she meekly (though with inner resentment) acquiesced. Indeed, the only resistance she ever showed to the new queen was in refusing to dismiss Sarah from her household.

Even when the crown finally came to Anne, the "shining moment," as she called it, it seemed to have come almost too late. In 1702 she was only thirty-six, but she already was stout, worn out by childbearing and so stricken with gout that she had to be carried about in a chair. She had become careless in her habits and appearance. Sir John Clark, a Scots commissioner, gives this appalling description of her only three years later:

> I was frequently at Kensington, and I twice saw her in her closet. Her Majesty was laboring under a fit of the gout and in extreme pain and agony, and on this occasion everything about her was much in the same disorder as about the meanest of her subjects. Her face, which was red and spotted, was rendered somewhat frightful by her negligent dress, and the foot affected was tied up with a poultice and some nasty bandages. What are you, poor mean-like mortal, thought I, who talks in the style of a sovereign?

Indeed, what use were palaces to one so discomforted? In the age that was to produce such prodigious structures as Blenheim and Castle Howard, Anne always preferred small, stuffy rooms where she could hide away from draughts and crowds with a few intimates. But she sought in vain to escape the rigors of her position. Her brother-in-law William had bequeathed her a horrible war that would last throughout her reign. To run it she was fortunate enough to have a great general, the greatest of his time, but the combination of John Churchill victorious in Flanders and Bavaria with Sarah ruling at court made the queen seem more than ever a puppet. If she demurred to a Whig appointment, Sarah might counter with a veiled reference to the horrid fate of Charles I. Parliament was unruly, pamphleteers libelous, and the Jacobites abroad were always calling down curses on Anne's head and plotting her assassination. Sometimes it must have seemed to the poor woman as if everyone were shouting at her!

Sarah must have seemed the loudest of all. Yet Sarah was fortunately more and more obsessed with her own domestic concerns and let weeks go by now without so much as turning up at court. Anne did not betray the smallest umbrage. She was totally unlike the Stuart men in the steadfastness of her

loyalty to friends. Her conferring of benefits on Sarah continued long after she had ceased to regard her as in any way a
true intimate. Indeed, from one letter to Godolphin it appears
that the queen had essentially given Sarah up as a friend as
early as 1704, a year before Blenheim and the supposed high-
water mark of the Marlboroughs' favor in court:

> I agree that all Lady Marlborough's unkindness pro-
> ceeds from ye real concern she has for my good, but
> I can't hope as you do, that she will ever be easy
> with me again. I quite despair of it now, which is no
> small mortification to me.

Anne had learned perfectly to conceal her feelings. But
they were there. First and foremost was her devotion to the
Church. Second was her devotion to her dynasty. She owed
her crown to Parliament, which had swept aside her half
brother's claim, but she never forgot that she was a granddaughter of the martyred Charles I and a great-granddaughter
of James I, the exponent of the divine right of kings. And
finally she abhorred cruelty and bloodshed. She had been appalled in Scotland by her father's use of the barbarous laws of
torture of that kingdom against recalcitrant nonconformists.
As queen she was constantly agonized by the brutal death
sentences that she had to sign, often adding little billets urging mitigation or commutation. It is to be noted that there
were no political executions in her reign. And from the beginning she regarded the slaughter of the war in Flanders and
Spain with a profound dismay and mistrust.

When Anne began to look about her to see what were her
resources, she found that they were considerable. In the first
place, she was popular. The people were happy to have an
English sovereign after Dutch William, and Anne was thoroughly English. As David Green has said: "Today, as a good-
humored woman, she would probably have enjoyed pottering
in her garden and giving her neighbors plants." In the second

place, she had a fine, musical voice, which delighted the groups she addressed. And even the grudging Sarah admitted that she had a person and appearance not ungraceful and that there was "something of majesty in her look." She could also be stubborn. She wrote to Godolphin: "Whoever of ye Whigs who thinks I am to be hectored or frightened into a compliance though I am a woman are mightily mistaken." And, finally, she was the monarch, still possessed of immense constitutional powers, including that of dissolving Parliament and selecting her ministers at will. It was not long before she learned that there were plenty of people who asked for nothing better than to help her fling the Whigs out of power. All she had to be sure of was that she would not be substituting one tyrant for another.

One of the early indications that Anne would not be a do-nothing sovereign was her reclaiming of the ancient but long-abandoned pretension to the power of healing. Seated in state in the banqueting chamber at Whitehall, surrounded by the great officers of her court, the queen would place white ribbons with pieces of "angel-gold" round the necks or on the arms of patients suffering from the "King's evil," the catch-all name given to diseases curable by the crown. One child brought to the cure grew up to be Dr. Samuel Johnson, who would always remember the lady "in diamonds and a long black hood." Sarah probably sneered at the procedure as the rankest superstition, but there was a woman of the queen's bedchamber who must have at least pretended not to.

Abigail Hill had taken to bringing her cousin, Robert Harley, a former speaker of the House of Commons and a leading Tory, privately to the queen's chambers. This process was facilitated when he became one of the two secretaries of state. It was thus that the great plan for stopping the European conflict was hatched. Anne hated war, as she hated the grim death warrants that she had so constantly to sign. Sarah by now had allowed herself to be offended too often and to show it too much. It was time to listen to Abigail and Harley. Perhaps there was something, after, all, that could be done.

There was probably no one crisis that catapulted Anne into the resolution that it would no longer be possible to govern England by acting as a moderator between two violent, contending parties; it was undoubtedly a long, slow process. But it is difficult not to imagine that the loneliness thrust upon her by the death of an ever-kindly, always affectionate, long-ailing husband in October 1708 and the almost simultaneous collapse into hatred of her long-deteriorating relationship with Sarah did not intensify her sense of isolated responsibility. When Louis XIV rejected the absurdly onerous terms of the Grand Alliance the following May, Anne was still willing to go along with the English war party, but probably only because, like Godolphin, she was persuaded that one more campaign could be counted on to finish off the exhausted French. Her misgivings, however, were profounder than ever, and she was surely alarmed when Marlborough, whom she had supported through thick and thin despite the ravings of his impossible wife, picked this moment to ask for a life appointment as captain-general. "Another Cromwell," Harley must have hissed in her ear. "King John," the Tories shrieked. Anne refused the commission and watched her general more closely than ever.

September 11, 1709, brought, not a final defeat of the French, but the bloody Allied victory of Malplaquet, where forty-five thousand soldiers were left dead on the field, nearly half of them Allied. "When will this bloodshed ever cease?" was the queen's anguished cry, which gave mortal offense to the war goddess Sarah. Once again the importunate Marlborough requested the life appointment and once again he was refused, but this time curtly.

The Whigs might even at this point have maintained control of the government had they in their arrogance not sought to impeach Henry Sacheverell, who, from his pulpit at St. Paul's, had attacked the validity of the revolution of 1688. The trial, attended by the queen herself, aroused great popular feeling against the Whigs, traditional backers of the revolution, and resulted in a nominal sentence against the clergyman. It might have been thought that the queen, who owed her crown to the revolution, would have been against Sacheverell, but she had always had a strong leaning to the Tories, and, as a true great-granddaughter of James I, she wanted to rule on a higher authority than the popular will. What she may have read in the tumult over the trial (and everyone agreed that she looked very pensive during it) was that the parties were more evenly and more passionately divided than she had supposed. And if that were true, might it not be time for the crown to take a stand?

As if to fortify and determine the queen in her slowly gathering resolution, some foolhardy Whigs decided this was the moment to debate the question of moving the House of Commons to petition the elimination of Mrs. Masham from the royal household. Anne was totally outraged. That her consoling bedchamber woman should be treated in the same fashion as Edward II's homosexual lover, Piers Gaveston, was the final insult. Harley cautioned her that it would be wise to make no move while a Whig Parliament was in session. Under the three-year act it could sit until the spring of 1711. But Parliament could always be prorogued (adjourned, as opposed to dissolved), and once prorogued, the queen could safely substitute Harley for Godolphin as lord treasurer. The shift of the treasury patronage could then be counted on to undermine the Whig electorate in only a few months' time, at which point the prorogued Parliament could be dissolved and a presumably Tory one elected. Anne could then fill out her cabinet with members of the antiwar faction, and negotiate a peace.

She bided her time until April. But when she struck, she

struck fast. On April 5, 1710, she prorogued Parliament. On April 6 she had her final interview with Sarah. Never again were the two women to meet, although Sarah in the years to come was to write countless letters and print hundreds of pages to establish her own rancorous version of the split. On April 10 the duke of Shrewsbury, a Whig but of Harley's faction, was raised to the office of lord chamberlain. On April 18 Marlborough was made to swallow the appointments of Abigail's husband and brother as colonels. And early in June, Marlborough's son-in-law, the earl of Sunderland, a man of republican sympathies whom the queen had always detested and whose appointment to her cabinet had represented the bitterest tea of Sarah's domination, was summarily dismissed.

Anne now paused for breath. She was reluctant to part with Godolphin, who had served her so long and well. He was, after all, "Mr. Montgomery," in the intimate correspondence with "Mr. and Mrs. Freeman" and "Mrs. Morley." She had always feared that if he went, Mr. Freeman would go with him, and she had tried, always ineffectually, to detach him from the dominating and possessive Mrs. Freeman. But now it seemed clear that there was no way of compromising with the Marlboroughs. If Anne was to have her peace, there was only one way to go about it. In August she sent word to Godolphin to destroy the staff of his office. Understandably, she wished to avoid the pain of a personal interview. Harley, soon to be raised to the earlship of Oxford and Mortimer, was now named lord treasurer and chief administrative officer of Britain.

In September Parliament was dissolved, and, as anticipated, a Tory landslide followed. The year 1711 witnessed the final liquidation of the Marlborough-Godolphin faction. In January Sarah was stripped of all her posts at court; eleven months later her husband was relieved of his command and ordered to answer an inquiry into his use of army funds. If this seems to modern eyes a harsh way of treating a general who had been guilty only of gaining prodigious victories for his country, let it be remembered that in Tudor days he would have probably lost his head for failing to retain the royal favor. All that now remained to do was to make peace, and early in 1712 Anne created twelve new peers, including Abigail's husband, to ensure a majority in the House of Lords to prevail against those intransigents who refused to consider any cessation of hostilities while Philip V was still on the Spanish throne.

But did Anne really do all this herself? Twentieth-century historians are reluctant to admit so much power in a crowned head. Let us put it this way, then: it could not have been done without her. Jonathan Swift had as great a grasp of what was going on as any political observer, and he consistently saw that the queen was the key. She could be manipulated, yes. But she *had* to be manipulated; that was the point. Swift was ruthless in the way he hounded those of the peace faction, Harley and Abigail, to be unwavering in their attendance on Anne. They were hardly to let her out of their sight! As soon as they did, they might be lost. And indeed, a few years later, Harley was.

The British Government now entered into negotiations for peace with France independently of its allies, a step that has been considered by many as the ultimate justification of the term "Perfidious Albion." The secret preliminaries between the two nations provided that Louis XIV would recognize Anne as *de jure* queen of Britain and acknowledge the Hanoverian, as opposed to the Stuart, succession to her crown. Dunkirk would be demilitarized. An Anglo-French commercial treaty would be signed. Britain would keep Gibraltar and Port Mahon and enjoy the same commercial privileges in Spain and France. A less edifying clause accorded to Britain the Spanish-American slave trade.

The terms once agreed upon, Britain simply walked out of the war. The duke of Ormonde, Marlborough's successor, was forbidden to engage in any further sieges or battles. The pay of all foreign troops was abruptly discontinued. Heavy casualties to England's allies resulted. There was a widespread feeling of shame among the Whigs; many considered that the national honor had been stained. But Anne had her peace. She might have muttered something about making omelets and breaking eggs.

Some modern historians, from Winston Churchill to Edward Gregg, have been of the opinion that Marlborough undeterred by Queen Anne and the Tories would have marched right into Paris and dictated the peace terms at Versailles. In this light Anne appears as a historical novelty: a monarch who leashed the greatest soldier of her nation's history in order to make less advantageous terms with her enemies than could have been obtained by the normal course of continued war; an early Talleyrand who feared the effects on her people of too sweeping a victory. But supposing this were the case, is Anne necessarily so much to blame? Perhaps she was wise. Too decisive a victory might have done some very strange things to that balance of power that British statesmen were already beginning to talk about. A prostrated France might have come back as threateningly as Germany or Russia in our own time. Britain, after all, had obtained all the commercial advantages that many of her business people regarded as the only excuse for prolonging the war, and Holland had gained immunity for a century from the threat of French invasion. Who cared whether a Bourbon or a Hapsburg sat on the throne in Madrid? Shouldn't most wars in history not have been fought at all? If fought, shouldn't they have been ended at the earliest possible moment?

In reassigning Sarah's posts, the queen followed a policy that was to guide her thenceforth to the end of her reign. She placed Abigail in charge of her privy purse, but she made the duchess of Somerset, wife of a great Whig peer who was also related to the royal family, mistress of the robes and groom of the stole. In this way she kept both parties guessing about her and could never again be taken for granted.

It worked. Abigail could not be sure, if she left the queen for a day—and she had to, poor woman, with her frequent pregnancies—that she would not find the duchess of Somerset monopolizing the royal favor on her return. Harley never knew what Whigs the queen might have been talking to, and the Jacobites were never sure whether the queen favored the Hanoverian or the Stuart succession. But if there was power in being a sphinx, there was also loneliness. Anne confided to Sir David Hamilton that she had no one to trust. Her health was collapsing. Her court was duller than ever.

At the end it seems incontestable that her thoughts kept turning to her young half-brother James, the pretender. How much preferable to leave the crown to her father's son rather than to the hated Hanoverian! But Anne remained a good member of the Church of England, and James Stuart spurned her hints that he abandon Catholicism. So there was nothing that could be done about it. James III might have been as good a monarch as George I, and Charles III as competent a one as George II (which is making no great claim for either), but they were not to have the chance.

Anne, like so many sovereigns, should never have been a chief of state. One pities her as one reads her wails: "What, do they think I'm a child and to be imposed on?" or "Why for God's sake must I, who have no interest, no end, no thought but for the good of my country, be made so miserable as to be brought into the power of one set of men?" Well, she escaped that power and ended a terrible war. Louis XIV in 1702, when informed that England had announced the opening of hostilities, remarked that he had to be getting old, when a woman declared war on him. He was being facetious, but it was that same woman who, a dozen years later, would save him from total defeat in the war that he had so rashly kindled.

XII

The English Succession and
the Electress of Hanover

One of the mysteries about ancient Rome is why a people whose particular genius was law should have been incapable of devising a system of orderly succession to the imperial crown. In the five centuries that elapsed between the establishment of the empire by Octavius Caesar and the death of its pathetic last sovereign, Romulus Augustulus, under a system that permitted the emperors to divide and subdivide the imperium at will and to adopt their successors, either within or without the imperial family, some seventy chiefs of state died violent deaths, and the average reign was five years. The Holy Roman Empire profited from the experience of its pagan predecessor by making its crown elective, chosen by the heads of certain German states and cities, and by limiting their choice (by tradition at least) to a member of the Hapsburg family.

France, early in its history, adopted a system even more chastely independent of the wishes and passions of her people. There the crown was limited by primogeniture to the male descendants of a king of France in a direct male line. So strictly was this rule adhered to that on the death of Henri III in 1589 and the extinction of the Valois line of the Capets, the crown passed to his remote cousin, Henri de Bourbon, even though the latter was a Protestant (he did, however, abjure) and even though he had to trace his line all the way back to Saint Louis (who died in 1270) to find the required royal ancestor.

In England the Salic rule barring descent through females was relaxed, and women were even deemed qualified to succeed to the throne, though this was for a long time disputed. On the death of Henry I his nephew Stephen prevailed over his daughter Maud in a civil war over the succession, but Maud's son was allowed to become king (Henry II) after Stephen. Much later the House of York claimed the crown (which eventually came to Henry VII as the consort of Elizabeth of York), not through their descent in a male line from the fourth son of Edward III, but through a female line from that monarch's second son. England did not have a queen regnant until Mary Tudor in 1553, but then it had two in succession, for Mary was succeeded by her half sister Elizabeth. Yet there was still a question whether these princesses took under ancient law or under the will of their father, Henry VIII. By the reign of James II (1685–88), however, it was fairly well established that his daughter Mary would succeed him in default of male issue. Unfortunately for the future of the orthodox tradition, a son and heir was born in what became the last year of his reign. James II and the infant son had to be sent packing before his throne could be offered to Mary.

As the English were determined not to endure another Catholic sovereign, it was necessary not simply to depose the king (there was plenty of precedent for that) but to alter permanently the rules of succession. A king could be deposed for arbitrary and despotic behavior (later called unconstitutional), but how could Parliament justify the nullification of an innocent infant's claim? Obviously an anti-Catholic rule had to be laid down, and it would have to cover all infants baptized Catholics. But suppose the excluded infant grew up and changed his religion? Or suppose he simply pretended to? People would be constantly claiming the throne. The only way to safeguard against this was to exclude all living Catholics and their posterity, regardless of future changes of faith. The succession could then be limited to known Protestants, with a provision for the disqualification of any of these who should thereafter be converted to Rome, or marry a Catholic.

It was not an easy thing to work out in a day when dynastic claims were considered sacred. When Louis XIV, in his one great deviation from his own principles, had endeavored to place his legitimated bastard sons in the line of succession to the crown, even he had not dared to place them ahead of the princes of the blood—that is, the male descendants in a direct male line from a king of France. All he had wanted to do was to anticipate the crisis that might arise on the extinction of the princes of the blood, at which point presumably an assemblage of the French peers (or the Estates-General?) would have to choose a new sovereign house. Louis had hoped to forestall such a crisis by making his beloved bastard, the duc du Maine, eligible to take the crown. The emergency was remote and never in fact occurred, as there were a good number of princes of the blood, but the mere idea that even an absolute monarch should presume to tamper with the succession caused great outrage (the duc de Saint-Simon simply boiled over), and as soon as the old king was dead his edict was rescinded.

James's daughter Mary accepted the offer of the English crown, but only on condition that her husband share it with her and rule alone if he survived. William did survive, and Anne had to wait until 1702 to become queen, deprived thus of six years of what, without parliamentary interference, should have been her reign. But she could hardly complain, as her own father was still living until a few months before William's death. And England was spared what might have been a grave constitutional crisis had William remarried and had a son. Under the new law that son would have come after Anne, but there might have been considerable confusion at the prospect of the king's sister-in-law taking precedence over a prince of Wales.

What it all boiled down to, of course, was that Parliament had made the crown elective, and it is elective to this day. A newspaper article that I read in 1981 suggested that as both the sovereign and the prime minister were now women, the first child of the prince of Wales should be his heir apparent even if that child should be a female and have a younger brother. This was not entirely fanciful. Parliament could so decree tomorrow. Just before the death of William III, Parliament, now convinced that neither the king nor Anne (who had lost seventeen children and was not of an age to have more) would die survived by issue, passed the Act of Succession, settling the crown, in that eventuality, on the electress Sophia of Hanover.

It is interesting to note what individuals living in 1701 were thus passed over. They made up a powerful group, more than forty in number. There was first, of course, James III, the Old Pretender, and his sister Louisa, exhausting (after Anne, brought up Protestant by order of Charles II) the issue of James II. After James II we turn to the issue of his sister, Henriette, duchesse d'Orléans. In 1701 these consisted of the duchess of Savoy, her two young sons, and her two married daughters, the duchesse de Bourgogne and the queen of Spain. This exhausts the issue of Charles I, and we turn next to the issue of James I, through his daughter Elizabeth, deposed queen of Bohemia.* In 1701 these consisted of Elizabeth Charlotte, duchesse d'Orléans (the second "Madame" who was a daughter of Elizabeth's son, Charles Louis), her two children and grandchildren; the three daughters of Edward, prince Palatine, son of Elizabeth, and their issue, which included some seventeen members of the House of Condé

---

* Her husband, Frederick V, elector of the Palatinate on the Rhine, had been elected king of Bohemia, but had lost both principalities in the Thirty Years' War. The Palatinate was later restored to his son.

and a future Holy Roman empress; Louise, abbess of Maubuisson, a daughter of Elizabeth; and finally, Elizabeth's youngest daughter, Sophia, widow of the elector of Hanover, then aged seventy-one. As she was the first undoubted Protestant in the list, the search stopped with her.

She accepted the offer gladly, but did not live to enjoy it. The crown devolved upon her son, George I, who could hardly speak English, cared little for his new kingdom and did not even have a queen, having locked up his wife for adultery. It is hard for us today to comprehend the logic of English thinking at the time. If Parliament, having skipped over forty names, had chosen to pass over Sophia and her issue, it would then have exhausted the issue of James I. As there were no other issue of James's mother, Mary queen of Scots, or of her father, James V of Scotland, or of his mother, Margaret Tudor, the next line to trace would have been that of Henry VIII's youngest sister, Mary Tudor, duchess of Brandon, which would have brought the search to the duke of Somerset, a prominent and capable English peer. Would he not have been preferable to the elector of Hanover? Evidently not. Parliament seems to have regarded itself as absolutely bound by its genealogical rule with the single exceptions of the Catholic exclusion and the special case of William III, promoted ahead of Anne in the succession, but what was left of a rule with loopholes of that size?

Sophia, at any rate, would have made an excellent queen of England. She was far abler than her son, and from the beginning she had played what looked like a poor hand of cards astutely. Not only did she help her husband, a younger son, to unite three duchies, Celle, Brunswick and Hanover, under his ultimate rule and to attain to the high rank of elector; she managed to ingratiate herself with the English and qualify for the succession to their throne without disturbing her friendship with the host of bypassed relatives. She was a realist as well as a diplomat. She was as firm and definite as any German royalty on all questions of rank and precedence, but she knew how to use the points involved for her own substantial advancement, and not, as in the case of Saint-Simon, for petty and inconsequential gains at court.

We catch an occasional glimpse of meanness in her memoirs, but there is always a reason for it. When on a trip to Italy she insisted acidulously on taking precedence over the amiable Madame de Colonna, we infer that she was really motivated by her husband's obvious interest in his old charmer. And the unlovably stern position that she took in the tragic case of her maltreated though adulterous daughter-in-law (incarcerated for life in a castle because of her affair with Koenigsmark) may have been related to a fear that the latter's tarnished reputation could have endangered the English succession. The electress was not going to have the work of a lifetime jeopardized by the carryings-on of a little tramp!

Queen Anne could never tolerate the idea of the Hanoverian succession, and Sophia's death, shortly before her own, certainly brought her no sadness. Tom Durfey, the queen's favored songwriter, who took his stand by the sideboard after her dinner to repeat the less obscene doggerel of the day, may have chanted this brutal rhyme to his royal patroness:

> *The crown's far too weighty*
> *For shoulders of eighty,*
> *She could not sustain such a trophy;*
> *Her hand, too, already*
> *Has grown so unsteady,*
> *She can't hold a scepter,*
> *So Providence kept her*
> *Away, poor old dowager Sophy!*

Sophia's niece Elizabeth Charlotte, princess Palatine—a big, plain, rough country girl who adored hunting and kept her rooms full of dogs—forms an amusing contrast to the aunt whom she adored and to whom she wrote voluminous letters. Elizabeth Charlotte made the worst of everything, just as Sophia made the best. She changed her religion to effect an advantageous marriage to the duc d'Orléans, brother of Louis XIV, but it cost her the English throne, to which she had the first claim after the Savoys. Then she had the misery of seeing her beloved Palatinate ravaged by her brother-in-law Louis's troops on the excuse of her own claim to it. She unsuccessfully resisted Louis XIV's plan to marry her son to one of his bastards, and she blotted her copybook with Madame de Maintenon by filling her letters (which she must have known would be read by palace spies) with every kind of obscene abuse of the king's morganatic spouse. And when her son finally became regent on the death of Louis XIV she allowed her disapproval of his dissolute life to spoil her pleasure in the supremacy that she had at long last attained.

And yet there is something lovable about "Madame." One's heart goes out to this honest, well-meaning tomboy married to a mean-minded homosexual who cared as much for jewelry and scent as she did for dogs, and who was placed in the impossible position of successor to his former wife, the lovely Henriette, adored by all the court. The second Madame is touchingly candid about her relations with Monsieur and the *modus vivendi* that they ultimately, more or less amicably, worked out. And one can see in the reckless way that she puts every bit of slander and gossip into her correspondence a way of getting back at an elegant and cruel court that was always sneering at her. But it is necessary to remember, in reading her letters, that she was hopelessly inaccurate. There is not a jot of evidence, for example, to show that Madame de Maintenon felt the slightest hostility to her.

The letters are a random jumble of anecdotes and complaints, and they make lively reading. She jots down whatever comes to mind. She tells of a woman who has lived to be a hundred and ten, and of an Indian who had a vision that somebody's brother had been killed in Canada at the very moment, as it later turned out, of the vision. A woman executed for murder has been warned to beware of a man bearing her surname, and lo and behold, the axman's name is the same as hers. Gospel truth! She complains of the spread of sodomy, of drunkenness among ladies of the court, and of the scandalous disregard for rank among the young. Her daughter-in-law is the laziest woman in Versailles, with the possible exception of her granddaughter. Marriage is a trap, court life a bore, the French hopelessly trivial; were it not for the hunt of the boar, stag or wolf, life would be hardly bearable. She cannot even go away to visit her daughter in Lorraine because the duke claims the right of equal armchairs with her, and the king will not hear of it. The war is frightful, because the poor Germans always get the worst of it. And, of course, Madame de Maintenon was, is and always will be, a bitch.

One's sympathy is ultimately a bit diminished by the realization that Madame was one of those people who really loved only those who were far away from her—that is, the recipients of her multitudinous letters. She shows little fondness for any of her descendants and is quite impersonal in describing their antics and follies. She could never, like her aunt the electress and the latter's daughter, the duchess of Brunswick, have corresponded with Leibniz. Madame appeals to us because Versailles gave her such a hard time, but had she been able to do it over to her own taste, it might not have appealed to us much more than the one she detested.

XIII
Madame de Maintenon

Madame de Maintenon retorted once to a lady at court who complained of having been slandered: "You worry about slander? What do you think we live on here?" She had become hardened to vituperation in a long, hard lifetime. And had she, poor woman, been able to look into the future, she would have seen that it would survive her for centuries. Even when her detractors have been contradicted, her defenders have rarely elevated her to much of a pedestal. She has never been a sympathetic character to historians in the past. At best they rated her a *dévote;* at worst, a hypocrite; and almost all of them considered her a prude.

An interesting reason for what today we should call Madame de Maintenon's "bad press" has been suggested by one of her biographers, Mme. Saint-René Taillandier: that all her life she found herself in false positions, and that people who constantly find themselves in false positions must expect to be called hypocrites. Yet they could be victims of coincidence.

From the very beginning, her social status was confused. Françoise d'Aubigné was born poor, the child of an imprisoned, debt-ridden, dissipated father and of the daughter of his jailer. Yet her paternal grandfather, Agrippa d'Aubigné, had been of noble lineage, a famous warrior and a friend of Henri

IV. The young Françoise always clung passionately to the grand-paternal memory. It was her sole dowry. As she retorted to another little girl of the prison garrison who boasted that her family's table service was of silver: "Ours may be of tin, but I'm a demoiselle, and you are not."

She was early taken from destitute parents and brought up in turn by different relatives, an orphan who was not really an orphan. Even her religious situation was muddled, for she was transferred from Protestant to Catholic aunts and subjected to vigorous proselytization on both sides. Agrippa d'Aubigné had been a famous Huguenot warrior, and had his loyal granddaughter ever known him, his persuasiveness might have been decisive. As it was, her ultimate conversion to the church of Rome was genuine and lifelong, but she reserved a stubborn conviction that a particularly beloved Protestant aunt would not be damned, and she always labored to convert her friends and relations in the other camp, working in the later days of her prosperity "for their fortune as well as their salvation." She would bear permanently the marks of the Huguenot faith. It has been noted, for example, that she never mentions the Virgin and rarely a saint in her correspondence, and there is a ring of reform in the constant emphasis that she places on the importance of good works and in her insistence that the religious education offered the girls at her convent school of St. Cyr should prepare them to be good wives and mothers.

To continue the outline of her ambivalence, at seventeen she was married to the middle-aged scatalogical poet and playwright Scarron, the wheelchair victim of a dozen repulsive ailments. So having been an aristocrat and a pauper, a daughter and an orphan, a Catholic and a heretic, she was now a wife and a virgin, subject, of course, to whatever private sexual practices her impotent husband may have demanded of her. The young Madame Scarron, however, made the best of a bad lot. She became a charming and tactful hostess to her invalid husband's brilliant but sometimes difficult friends and performed a daily miracle of the loaves and fishes with his slender means. When Scarron died, his widow was already a known figure in Paris intellectual and social circles—witty, practical, discreet, well but simply dressed, excellent company, with the clearest, smoothest skin and bright black eyes.

There was no money, of course, except for a small pension accorded by the queen mother, Anne of Austria, at the urging of powerful friends, but this problem was soon to vanish. Louis XIV and Madame de Montespan were looking for just the right person to raise in secrecy their growing family of royal bastards. The children were to be kept out of sight until of age because of the possibility that Madame de Montespan's husband, crazed with jealousy, might claim custody out of spite. The job of running a large nursery in the daytime and of continuing imperturbably at night a social life that would throw people off the track was not an easy one to fill. But Madame Scarron seemed made to order for it, and, after long, serious sessions with her confessor about how God felt on the question of educating the king's illicit issue, she accepted.

The marquise de Maintenon, as she was soon promoted to be, became genuinely devoted to the royal offspring and saw them, of course, far more than did their dazzling but preoccupied mother. And now opened still another ambivalent role: the mother who was no mother. She was to play it for a decade, and it would be the threshold for her advance to the ultimate false position: the queen who was no queen. Sometime in 1685, two years after the death of queen Marie-Thérèse, Louis XIV was secretly wed to the governess of his natural children. Until his death thirty years later she would be the uncrowned queen of France.

And even in the next reign there was to be a final mask. In 1715 Madame de Maintenon retired to St. Cyr, and for the last four years of her life she was directress of her convent school, an abbess who was no abbess. When Peter the Great barged into her chamber and yanked aside the curtains of her bed to stare at this creature of mystery, the most direct and the most indirect of human beings contemplated each other for a moment of silence.

It is easy to see that many people would not believe that a person capable of playing so many roles could be possessed of much sincerity, but it should be remembered that most of these roles were forced upon her, and that she played them all brilliantly. She tidied up old Scarron's life and made his salon work. She supplied the royal bastards with the only home they were ever to know, and she provided her mighty sovereign, who chose to wear the world on his shoulders, with a place where he could both work and take his ease, giving him a confidante who could listen, sympathetically and eternally, to his problems. And finally she offered an excellent education and a chance of marriage to unendowed girls of good family who would otherwise have been locked up for life in a convent.

Why then should she be so unpopular? Perhaps it is simply that it was hard to conceive that she could have been honest in stating as often as she did that she had neither sought nor enjoyed her great position. Louise de La Vallière was genuinely in love with the king, and Athénaïs de Montespan was genuinely in love with his glory; both found satisfaction in being his mistress. But Françoise de Maintenon was never in the least in love with the king. She found sexual intercourse (which continued until both were in their seventies) tedious, and her husband's self-absorption rebuffing. She was exhausted by the rigors of life in Versailles ("We perish in symmetry," she moaned) and bored by the demands of the royal family. Glory had come to her too late; she was already fifty when the king married her, and she attributed the sole motivation of her arduous existence to her conviction that God had given her the job of saving Louis' soul and of promoting the interests of his church. I find Madame de Maintenon much more credible at her own valuation than at those of her critics. I see her as a deeply religious person who half (but only half) reluctantly accepted the demand that she believed her God had made of her to take charge of the spiritual destinies of her sovereign and his family of bastards. And I find this perfectly consistent with the moments of elation that her dizzying social status must have afforded to a nature that was not, after all, altogether unworldly.

Let us examine the testimony of her two principal contemporary detractors. The fiercest was the duc de Saint-Simon. Be it observed that he never laid eyes on her until the sixteen-nineties, when she was over seventy, and that she hardly ever spoke to him. But of course he *heard* everything about her and made notes of what he heard. According to him she had been a lady of many intrigues in the old Scarron days, and her religious devotion was nothing but a cover for her violent ambition to dominate the king and create a political future for the royal bastards for whom she had a frustrated mother's frantic devotion. But even Saint-Simon had to admit that for a woman so taken up with the world, she spent a great deal of time on church matters:

> Usually, as soon as she arose, she went straight off to Saint-Cyr and ate, either alone or with a favorite nun, gave as few audiences as possible, presided over the convent's internal affairs, regulated the church, read and answered letters, directed the convent schools in all parts of France, received reports from her spies, and returned to Versailles almost exactly at the time when the king habitually visited her.

He adds that her mornings, which began very early, were filled by interviews with "obscure persons concerned with charities or religious administration." If Madame de Maintenon was indeed a hypocrite, she took extraordinary pains to play her role well. Saint-Simon wrote a magnificent account of the court of the Sun King, but how much of it is history and how much fiction remains a matter of serious concern to all students of the period. It seems to me impossible to read through the hundreds of letters that Madame de Maintenon left—not one of which was presumably ever read by Saint-Simon—and reconcile the writer with the monster of ego that emerges from the little duke's memoirs.

The second "Madame," Elizabeth Charlotte of Bavaria, duchesse d'Orléans, is vitriolic in her letters about Madame de Maintenon in much the same manner as Saint-Simon, but her bias is clear: she adored the king and, like all German royalties, was obsessed with rank and the horrors of misalliance. The daily vision of the discreet, silent, morganatic spouse, constantly closeted with the sovereign and his ministers, was anathema to one who was probably herself half in love with her royal brother-in-law and who certainly did not relish the presence of the "widow Scarron" in the bosom of the royal family.

The question of Madame de Maintenon's sexual promiscuity, so emphasized by these two detractors, is really important only in that it bears on the more interesting question of her alleged hypocrisy. For if she was really the "old trot" of Madame's rough phrase, she must have been truly a female Tartuffe to have devoted so many thousands of words, written and spoken, to the cult of the virtuous female.

In dealing with the charge, we may start with the assurance that neither the king nor his morganatic spouse committed adultery during the three decades of their marriage. It would have been almost impossible for either of them, watched as they were, to have got away with it. Besides, the king, who had no need for privacy, had never made any but the most perfunctory effort to conceal his affairs. Of course, it is true that both were getting older, but they continued, as already indicated, to make love until almost the end. The important point is that no observer in that attentive, gossiping court even suggested that the king or his wife had strayed.

Which brings us back to the time of Madame Scarron's marriage and widowhood. Did she have affairs in Scarron's lifetime? It has not been seriously claimed. Afterward? It has certainly been alleged that she did, but there is no evidence that I have been able to find except the unreliable statement of the ribald old Ninon de Lenclos made years later, when the subject of it had become famous, that Madame Scarron used to meet a certain gentleman in a bedroom in Ninon's house. What about her relations with the king before marriage? Jean Cordelier wrote a whole book to support the thesis that she became Louis' mistress during the life of the queen and suffered for the rest of her days from a guilty conscience. I suppose this is possible. It could have been the one affair of Louis' lifetime that he cared to hide—not so much from the court or the queen as from the violent, scene-making Madame de Montespan. And yet what made the latter far more jealous than any mere adultery was the protracted conversations *à deux* that went on between the king and his children's governess, witnessed but never overheard by the courtiers. Madame de Sévigné refers to these talks in her letters to her daughter. What were they talking about, so long and so earnestly?

Obviously Madame de Maintenon must have offered Louis something that no other woman had ever offered him. He had probably never really talked with a woman before. This sober, intelligent, sympathetic governess must have understood whatever it was that was bothering this essentially lonely man. He had been monarch since the age of four. He had never known his father, and there is nothing to indicate that Anne of Austria was a close mother. As a child he probably resented her minister-lover, Mazarin, and he certainly objected to her later attempts to deny him any extramarital love life. His wife was his mother's own niece and a fellow Spaniard, which made them almost allies against him. When he established at last his right to rule, both himself and his kingdom, and when he elected to love as he chose, he found many satisfactions but no real friends. His state was too grand. Yet there was still God. Religion taught him that even kings could be damned. What was he to do about the state of his own soul?

I suggest that this was the subject of his long conversations with the governess. Certainly he did not talk about *her* soul; Louis was interested only in himself, or in France as an extension of that self. And no father of his era would have talked at such length about his children. Leaving politics and war aside, as topics appropriate only for men and ministers, what was there left but the subject, a favorite one of the era, of soul saving? And I further suspect that Madame de Maintenon gave him the only advice that a devout Catholic could have given him: that he would have to give up adultery to be sure of salvation. She has been accused of treachery to Madame de Montespan in this, but that would only have been the case had she slept with the king. She might, I suppose, have offered him a kind of *amitié amoureuse.* And I have no doubt that, liking to please, she made him feel that his masculine charm would be actually enhanced by a return to virtue.

There are other reasons that she might not have been his mistress. The queen delighted in her friendship and gave her full credit for the king's renewed uxorial attentions. Is it likely that Louis would have gone back to his middle-aged wife at the suggestion of a mistress? And wouldn't Madame de Maintenon, by yielding to his advances, have destroyed her principal hold on his mind and heart: namely, his faith in her as a redeemer? It was the premature and totally unexpected death of the queen in 1683 that changed her whole picture. *Now* Françoise could be asked to look after Louis' body as well as his soul. She perhaps had not bargained for this; there is her own word that she did not like it. But the king had to have a woman and had to save his soul, and there seemed to be only one way that this could be accomplished: in a marriage to the person who had converted him to the virtuous life.

It is interesting that Louis, so amorous in his younger years, so keenly appreciative of female beauty, should have remained satisfied for the rest of his days with an elderly partner who took no pleasure in the act. It may be permissible to suspect that he was as much an egoist in love as in his other relationships, and that, once having satisfied himself, it never occurred to him that there was anyone else to satisfy. It is also possible that after 1685, when he had his upper teeth removed, and 1686, when he had his fistula operation, both of which ordeals visibly aged him, he was less sexually exigent.

After the secret marriage, of which all the world was aware, the king worked out the details of his new wife's position. It was to be unique. As Madame de Sévigné put it to her daughter, "There has never been anything like the position of Madame de Maintenon, and there never will be." What she meant was that no woman had ever been treated as a queen, and given all the respect and reverence of that position, without the slightest elevation of rank. In court, at receptions, in chapel, Madame de Maintenon took her rank as a simple marquise. Even Saint-Simon admits that she never exceeded this. If her heart swelled a bit as the ex-queen of England appeared to deprecate her modesty in stepping back, if her quick head shake and renunciatory smile concealed a tense satisfaction at majesty's recognition of the rank she *might* have taken, well, she was only human, wasn't she? In her own chamber, on the other hand, where the king spent many hours a day and where he conferred with his ministers, she was tacitly recognized as the royal spouse, and she gave instructions and advice to the king's children and grandchildren as if they were her own. She always remained a bit the governess, too, and it was not uncommon to see princesses of the blood leave her room with red eyes after a severe dressing down. In time she came to confine herself more and more to her chambers and to the convent school of St. Cyr that she had founded for girls, like herself of yore, of good birth but no dowry. She thus maintained her own tiny court in the heart of the great one, but the great one, as she well knew, passed its days listening at the door of the smaller.

It was inevitable that this mysterious priestess, robed in simple black velvet and wearing but a single ornament, a jeweled cross given her by the king, in whose rooms the monarch performed the tasks of the day, should have been credited with enormous influence. Imagine what we should say today if the President of the United States should confine himself to such an ambience! Some French historians have held her responsible for the revocation of the Edict of Nantes, the return of religious persecution and the military disasters and economic ruin that beset the end of the reign. There has always been a Gallic tendency to idealize the Sun King; Madame de Maintenon has been a convenient scapegoat on whom to blame the calamities of his administration. But there is not the slightest evidence that she ever wished to harm a Protestant or invade a neighboring nation.

If she had real political power, she must have had goals. But what changes did she seek to bring about? Anyone who pores through her immense correspondence is struck by her absorption in matters of religion and religious administration. She could not have had much time to care about taxes or economics or even wars. True, she was willing to help the king whenever he requested her aid, as in maintaining her long correspondence with the princesse des Ursins in Madrid, but her true joy was in the exercise of her remarkable administrative gifts in the running of convent schools. Life at court basically bored her, as it has bored many intellectuals. There was occasional excitement at Versailles, of course—how could there not be, in the center of world power?—but she preferred St. Cyr. After the king's death she never once returned to his great gilded palace.

Once one has dispelled the myths about Madame de Maintenon and settled down to enjoy her, there is considerable pleasure to be derived. She was a worthy friend of Madame de Sévigné. Her letters, which Napoleon preferred to the latter's, do not have the same charm of observation or phrasing, but they provide a feeling, at times almost a modern comment on the terrible events of the day. She strips Versailles of its glamor; she goes straight to essentials. She is never impressed with the great world. She is never vulgar. She has left us a vivid description of a typical day in her life at court, one that did not happen to start, as in Saint-Simon's account, with a visit to St. Cyr.

Her first caller arrives at half-past seven: the king's surgeon. She does not tell us what he does to her; perhaps he simply takes her pulse and looks at her tongue. He is followed by the great Fagon, the king's physician, who inquires more minutely about her health. There may then be just enough time to answer a few urgent letters before the more important callers: a minister, an archbishop, a general. Then comes her darling, the king's oldest bastard son, the duc du Maine (presumably a pleasant visit), who stays until the arrival of his father. Majesty will not depart until it is time to go to mass; poor Madame de Maintenon is not dressed yet. Had she taken time out for that, she assures us, she would not have been able even to say her prayers!

We deduce that she has dressed while the king is at mass, for he comes to her again immediately afterward. No sooner has he gone than the duchesse de Bourgogne, the Dauphin's daughter-in-law, arrives with her noisy, chattering ladies. Like a bunch of schoolgirls, they bring with them a host of little problems and petty squabbles that have to be adjusted and worked out. They regard Madame de Maintenon, we gather, as a kind of beloved headmistress or mother superior. They are eager to be of personal assistance, rushing about the chamber in an ineffective way to fetch her a book or a scarf or a pin. But really, one good valet would be vastly preferable to the bunch of them!

At last the ladies are off to their dinner, and she has a moment for a bite to eat with two ill friends who are brought in to share it with her. This would normally have been followed by a chance for a quick game of trictrac, but no. Monseigneur (the Dauphin) chooses this moment for his call (he has dined early, ahead of the others, because he is going hunting), and she must make weary small talk for an hour with this dullest of small talkers. By the time he leaves, the king's dinner is over, and in comes Majesty again, now accompanied by the princesses of the blood, and the room is filled once more with heat and noise. The king leaves after only half an hour, but not so the princesses. They linger on to gossip and shriek with laughter, demanding all of their hostess' attention though her heart may be heavy with some private grief or public disaster. And even after it is time for them to go, there is always one to remain behind, to insist on a private chat, to assail Madame de Maintenon with tales of domestic calamities and pleas for help.

When the king returns from the hunt, he is closeted alone with her, and she is at last spared further company. But then she must smooth all his worries and agitations. Louis can weep; yes, God can weep, when the doors are closed! But he has "no conversation," as she puts it, except for his own concerns. He certainly doesn't want to hear about *hers*. This is perhaps not really his fault. A naturally unimaginative man, rigidly trained from childhood in perfect egotism, is not easily made aware of other people's troubles.

Now it is time for work. A minister comes in to confer with the king. His wife, seated apart, has time for a few prayers, but she must be always ready for a question. And courtiers are admitted from time to time to announce what always seems to be disastrous news from the military front. A private supper is served to her at this time, but if the king wishes to show her a document or something on a map he does not hesitate to interrupt her hurried meal.

Finally, when she is so exhausted that even Louis, who never seems to tire, notices it, he suggests that she go to bed. But then he comes to sit by her, with the result that no servants can be present to warm her sheets or attend to her bodily wants (we must remember that she is an old woman and has not a "glorious physique"). Louis, who can sit in a carriage for hours without needing to empty his bladder, of course hasn't the faintest idea that she might need anything. He stays until it is time for his own supper, but even then her ordeal is not quite over. The Dauphin, with the duc and duchesse de Bourgogne, make a noisy entry to bid her good night. At ten o'clock she is left alone to sleep, if sleep she can, with her mind full of the horror of the latest military dispatches.

The woman so beset was not without her own loyal following, who saw her as a beacon light of faith and charity in the dark world of court intrigue. Far removed from the animosity of Saint-Simon or the jealousy of the duchesse d'Orléans is this tribute from a friend:

> And so now, every time that I shall see you pass, in that great black cape that envelops you like a cloud, I shall try to believe that you are reading in my heart the prayers that I shall be uttering that you may continue to enjoy for many years and in happier times the pleasure of doing good and of supporting the deserving wherever they may be found —for that is the only reward that is worthy of you.

Madame de Maintenon maintained an extensive correspondence with younger women who had either taken the veil or were contemplating the step, and she discussed frankly and sincerely her own religious problems to help them to solve theirs. I detect no note of Tartuffe in the following:

> Can't you see that I perish of sadness in a life of unimaginable greatness and that only God's help sustains me? I have been young and well favored; I have tasted many pleasures and had many loving friends; I have enjoyed the play of wit, and been graced by royal favor, yet I promise you, dear daughter, that all of these states have left me in a hideous void, nervous, exhausted, and pining for something else.

French literature owes a great debt to her for persuading Racine to take up the dramatist's pen that he had purported to drop forever and to compose *Esther* and *Athalie* for the girls at St. Cyr. Like her friends, Mesdames de Sévigné and de La Fayette, Madame de Maintenon had excellent taste in both poetry and prose, but as time went on and as she drew even closer to her church, she began to share Racine's own doubts about the validity of art and to approach the mystic position that nothing matters but the soul's union with God. The following censure of a young woman's supersensitivity in literary appreciations seems to end by questioning the importance of these very appreciations:

> How do you expect to rise above the trials that God will set for you if you are put off by a Norman or a Picardy accent, or if you are disgusted with an artist less sublime than Racine? He would have inspired you, poor man, had you seen his humility at the end. I saw another beautiful spirit die, who had written the most beautiful works a man can write and who wouldn't publish them, not wishing to be a

mere author. He burned them all. Only a few frag-
ments remain in my memory.

This begins to abut the extreme position that there is nothing but vanity outside the love of God. A sublime tragedy, a
comedy, a farce, a circus . . . is it worth distinguishing between them?

> I see the world in all its ugliness, while the trivial-
> minded are dazzled by it. I see the passions, the
> treasons, the baseness, the limitless ambitions, the
> envy, the rage, the willingness to destroy other hu-
> mans for trifles. I should be glad to go to the end of
> the world, even back to America (she had been as a
> child to Martinique) if I were not constantly re-
> minded that God wants me here. . . . I fear for
> the salvation of the king. . . . The operas, for ex-
> ample, that he so loves, but which are full of anti-
> Christian sentiments, should certainly be stopped or
> censored. But when I speak of it to him, he simply
> answers: "We have always had them."

This last, I admit, begins to strike the note of the religious
bigot; one can see why Madame de Maintenon was not popular with the young people at court. But her narrowness in
matters of entertainment need not blind us to her vision and
wisdom in larger matters, particularly in war.

I find her at her best and most sympathetic in her correspondence with the princesse des Ursins. As this remarkable
lady is the subject of the next essay, suffice it to say here that
as camarera-mayor, or principal lady of the bedchamber, to
the queen of Spain she dominated the royal couple and was
supposed to be acting as a French agent in Madrid. In fact,
her sympathies became entirely pro-Spanish, and when it began to look as if Louis XIV might abandon the cause of his

grandson and pull out of Spain, she became very shrill indeed. But Madame de Maintenon, whom some historians call a defeatist but whom I call a humane realist, could not see that it was proper to sacrifice Frenchmen for a Spanish cause and for what she believed a lost cause, at that.

Nothing shows more clearly her political powerlessness than these letters. She kept it up at the request of the king and his ministers, who wanted a firsthand report of what was going on in the court in Madrid, but she made no secret of her profound misgivings about the war. Like Queen Anne across the Channel she deplored the bloodshed and the waste; she seems at times like a wailing chorus from another era, perhaps our own, bemoaning the hideous futility of the carnage. She writes, at the close of 1708:

> You are quite right to say, Madame, that we must look at all our disasters as coming from God. Our king was too glorious; God must now wish to abase him in order to save him. France was overextended, perhaps improperly, so God may now wish to confine us to narrower boundaries; we may be stronger so. Our country was insolent and unruly; God is punishing us. But in *your* case, Madame, I see the issue less clearly; *your* king is virtuous; his cause is founded in justice; he was called to his throne by his people and named the true heir by his predecessor . . . his queen is an honor to her sex . . . that all *this*, Madame, should be offensive to God, I cannot fathom, but no doubt He will make it clear one day.

Madame des Ursins was not for a minute distracted by these compliments, although she acknowledged them warmly. She saw, quite correctly, in her friend's breast-beating the desire for peace, a separate peace if necessary, and she immediately feared that this might reflect official policy. To some extent it did. When she taxed her correspondent with this, the latter replied:

> Our differences of opinion must not cause us to quarrel. You think we should die rather than surrender; I think we should yield to superior force, as a sign from God, who is clearly against us. I believe that the king owes more to his people than to himself. But I can say this because no one listens to me. It is not I who will decide the issue between peace and war.

Her last statement was true. She might agree with the peace policy—she had always been against the war—but she was hardly its proponent. At any rate, she could reproach Madame des Ursins with lack of patriotism:

> Here is how things are, Madame. The king and queen of Spain have every reason to love you; the passion that you have for them has made you cease to be a French woman. We must pardon you and pray God that it may please him to alter your state.

But when the war was ended, and the princesse des Ursins, as we shall see, had been hounded from the Spanish court, when Louis XIV himself was finally dead, Madame de Maintenon replied with a serene nobility to the letter of condolence of her now humbled old friend:

> It was good of you, Madame, to think of me in the momentous period that has just passed. We can only bow our heads, under the hand that has struck us. I wish with all my heart that your state was as fortunate as mine. I have seen the king die like a saint and a hero. I have quit a world for which I never cared and am now in a retreat that is all my heart's desire.

And when Madame de Maintenon herself died four years later, her niece, Madame de Caylus, wrote to her secretary, Mlle. d'Aumale (two women who knew her intimately and totally admired her):

> You must spend the leisure hours, which now will not fail you, writing of the great events of her life. We shall review them together; it will be our consolation to recall what we have seen, and her modesty will no longer keep us from talking. We shall render to her glory all that we owe it.

XIV
Queen Christina, the Corneille Heroine

Sven Stolpe, in his life of Christina of Sweden, quotes from the posthumous work of Giovanni Papini, *The Last Judgment*, where the angel of justice harangues the spirit of the unfortunate queen in these harsh terms:

> People thought you a curious character, Christina of Sweden. You abandoned your father's faith, and struggled all your life long to gain other crowns, but in vain. You abjured your father's religion and attached yourself to the Catholic Church, but you brought shame on your conversion, since a little later you became the lover of a cardinal, and caused the murder of one of your favorites. People were more than indulgent with you, but now it will avail you nothing that you were beautiful, that you were a queen, a scholar and a poet. Now you are to be called to account for your crimes.

It is certainly true that Christina abandoned the Lutheran Church of her father, and that she sought without success the thrones of Naples and Poland after renouncing her Swedish one, and that she became a Roman Catholic. But the rest of the commination is but partly true. She probably was never the lover of Cardinal Azzolino, though due more to the physical aversion of that prelate than to her virtue, and although she certainly murdered Rinaldo Monaldeschi, he was not a favorite but a servant. And finally she was neither a beauty, a scholar, nor a poet. But perhaps some mercy should be extended to her, for in an era where the heroines of Pierre Corneille were all the vogue, she did her desperate best to become one.

Poor Christina! The daughter of Gustavus Adolphus, the lion of the north, should have been a Boadicea, a Penthesilea, a Zenobia, and not have ended as the sorry caricature of a warrior queen, the eagle turned into a goose, and a rather bloody goose at that.

Of course, it must be confessed that the great ladies of Corneille's tragedies, for whom the Francophile Christina had such an abiding admiration, are, at least by modern standards, an unlovable lot. They are arrogant and pompous to the point of seeming at times absurd, and they try to make it their glory to promote the pursuit of naked political power as the only fitting goal for a person of noble or royal birth. Yet at the same time they are subject to fits of violent jealousy which can turn them into vixens. It is difficult in some scenes to believe that their creator is not making fun of them. But he most certainly is not. Despite his comedies, Corneille had little sense of humor.

The proud Roman princess Honorie in *Attila* is willing to yield her disdainful hand to the Hun king because he has conquered the world, but she pulls it back fast enough when she discovers that his heart belongs to one she deems her social inferior. The Carthaginian princess Sophonisbe, in the tragedy of that name, boasts that she gains as great a satisfaction in taking a lover away from a rival as in gaining his love for herself, and Viriate, queen of Lusitania in *Sertorius*, declaims that liberty means nothing in a world that is free, that the sight of a neighbor in chains is what gives it all its value.

Their pride seems informed with vanity, their anger with pique.

Yet Corneille's magnificent language endows them with a certain loftiness; one does not quite snicker at their passion for rule. The wicked Cléopâtre in *Rodogune*, who is willing to sacrifice both her sons to retain the crown for which she has already committed many crimes, exclaims:

> *"Dût le peuple en fureur pour ses maîtres nouveaux*
> *De mon sang odieux arroser leurs tombeaux,*
> *Dût le Parthe vengeur me trouver sans défense,*
> *Dût le ciel égaler le supplice à l'offense,*
> *Trône, à t'abandonner je ne puis consentir;*
> *Par un coup de tonnerre il vaut mieux en sortir."*

Cléopâtre is evil, but a related sentiment is expressed by the virtuous Pulchérie in her eponymous piece, when, succeeding to the imperial throne in Constantinople, she banishes love forever from her heart:

> *"Je suis impératrice, et j'étais Pulchérie.*
> *De ce trône, ennemi de mes plus doux souhaits,*
> *Je regarde l'amour comme un de mes sujets;*
> *Je veux que le respect qu'il doit à ma couronne,*
> *Repousse l'attentat qu'il fait sur ma personne."*

The question that must now occur to the reader of these lines is how could a Corneille devotee like Christina do the one thing that none of his heroines would ever have done, for God or man or Satan? How could she give up a throne? How could she justify to herself an abdication that represented the very negation of all that the great playwright had purported to admire?

The answer must be sought in Christina's lofty definition of "virtue" in the classical, medieval and Renaissance sense, as representing excellence in every form. To her it was a kind of continuing test through the ages: one had to do better than

the classic heroes of antiquity. And the greatest heroes to her
were essentially just that: males. A woman could be great only
insofar as she made herself male. When people extolled
Christina as Sappho or a tenth muse, she complained that
they didn't have to remind her that she was a woman—she
knew it all too well! She insisted that she liked men not so
much because they were men as that they were *not* women,
and as late as 1680, when she was in her fifties, she actually
believed that she was turning into a man!

Sven Stolpe expresses ingeniously the way the concept of
abdication may have come to her as the ultimate challenge of
virtue:

> During her final period in Sweden, when half Eu-
> rope was honoring her as Queen of Peace, the Pallas
> Athene of the North, a Diana of pure virtue, she
> believed every word of it and seriously imagined her-
> self to be someone very special and unique in his-
> tory. Only the great heroes of antiquity, Cyrus, Al-
> exander, were her equals. She liked to rank these
> heroes high above her father, Gustavus Adolphus,
> but believed she surpassed them in one respect: one
> sacrifice they never made, the greatest of all: the
> sacrifice of themselves. Now Christina did not use
> the term in a Christian sense, it was not for love of
> God or man that she wanted to sacrifice herself, but
> for love of virtue: she wanted to do something unut-
> terably noble and be the greatest figure in history.
> Her special sacrifice would be to offer her privileged
> state, her crown, her country: she alone was in a
> position to do this. She believed—and did not mind
> saying—that she was among the most favored of all
> created beings. She had settled the problem of love,
> and the conduct of her private life, in what she
> considered a noble way, never giving way to a lower

instinct or a selfish urge. The ultimate proof was, however, still lacking, but born to be "queen with absolute power of the most famous nation in the world," she would accomplish what no one else had ever done before, she would eschew human greatnesses in order to achieve a unique inner greatness.

Who in European history before had abdicated but Diocletian and Charles V, and had both of them not been old?

The sad tale begins, as in so many others of her time, with an appalling youth. She was born in 1626, the only child of Gustavus Adolphus, the warrior monarch of the north, and of his neurotic, self-pitying, vapid spouse, Maria Eleonora of Brandenburg, and when she was only six her father's corpse was found, alone and stripped, on the battlefield of Lützen, of which he had been, nonetheless, the glorious victor. The Swedish king had been enticed into the war against the forces of the Holy Roman Emperor by the wily diplomacy of Cardinal Richelieu, who had not hesitated to bolster the Protestants in Germany against the Hapsburgs of Vienna and Madrid who threatened to encircle France. Richelieu's policy guaranteed the continuation of the horrors of German civil war for the full period of its titular three decades. After all, were the civilian populations of France or Sweden in any danger of slaughter or rapine? Who in Paris or Stockholm cared about the devastation of a war that C. V. Wedgwood has described as "morally subversive, economically destructive, socially degrading, confused in its causes, devious in its course, futile in its result . . . the outstanding example in European history of meaningless conflict"?

The war was to dominate the greater part of Christina's reign: sixteen of its twenty-two years. To do her justice, she was on the side of those who yearned for peace, but this did her little good against a regency council dominated by her father's belligerent old counselor, Axel Oxenstierna. The young queen, pale with fair hair hanging to her shoulders and a nervous, serious face dominated by a broad forehead and the prominent paternal nose, could do little more than watch her elders make their mistakes.

She was always very much alone. She had lost her father too young to miss him; later she was cynically to observe: "Children who await the succession of a crown are easily consoled for the loss of a father." It was indeed a fine thing to be "Queen of the Swedes, Goths and Vandals, Great Princess of Finland, Duchess of Estonia and Karelia and Lady of Ingria." The only person she had to obey at home was her neurotic and at times hysterical mother, but after two years Oxenstierna removed her from that dowager's inept hands and put her in the care of her father's more sensible sister Catherine, who had married John Casimir, Count Palatine. The resentful Maria Eleonora, kept a virtual prisoner by the regency council, succeeded at last in escaping to Denmark and then to Brandenburg, and she did not return to Sweden for nine years, by which time her daughter was grown up and free of her influence.

Christina was a very masculine young woman. At birth she was so hairy that she was first thought to be a boy. She was strong, and could sit for ten hours in the saddle at a hunt, but she suffered from violent abdominal pains, probably gastric colitis. The fact that one shoulder was lower than the other and that she paid scant attention to her dress and later took to wearing men's wigs and sometimes men's clothes did not enhance her charm. And her manners were abrupt to the point of rudeness. She was kind enough to servants, but in a familiar way that made them nervous, and she was easily bored. While still a ward of the regency council she coached her ladies to sing a filthy soldiers' ditty to the French ambassador in his own tongue. Stolpe is of the opinion that she was unattractive to both sexes, and it seems only too probable.

On the other hand, she was keenly interested in art and

scholarship and learned to speak some eight languages. Intelligent and intellectually curious, she was determined that if she could not dominate the politics of her country she could at least provide it with cultural superiority. It was with delight that she opened the looted treasures from Prague: canvases of Titian, Veronese, Correggio, Tintoretto, and hung them in her palaces. It was probably this collection that first persuaded her that Italy must be heaven compared to bleak Sweden. She built up a huge library; she organized elaborate ballets; she produced French plays. She invited painters and philosophers from all over Europe to her court. Oh, she would be as splendid as Solomon!

But who was to guide her? How could she ever develop any real sense of proportion? How could she be expected to distinguish between such butterflies as the Comte and Comtesse de Brégy, who brought all the latest polish and frivolity from Paris to dazzle royal eyes that wanted only too much to be dazzled, and René Descartes, whose visit to her court was considered by all Europe the peak of her achievements? She couldn't. It is sad to relate that the first philosopher of Europe was asked to compose verses for "The Triumph of Peace," a ballet organized to celebrate the treaty just signed at Westphalia! When the disgusted sage, who had told people that the queen knew nothing whatever of philosophy, sickened and died of congestion of the lungs in that cold northern clime, the learned world excoriated his hostess. But she had behaved only as countless other royalties have behaved. In much the same way, a few years later, she lost the chance of becoming a friend of the Prince de Condé, whose military genius she immensely admired, by keeping him standing before her armchair, even though it had been agreed that he had called upon her as a private person.

I believe that Stolpe has divined the true reason for Christina's abdication in 1654 at the age of twenty-eight, but it was neither of the two more commonly ascribed to her by contemporaries: her reluctance to marry and her desire to become a Catholic.

Her sex life has been the subject of many learned volumes and much lurid gossip. It seems evident to me that she had strong inclinations for both sexes, but that she probably had physical relations only with her own. She was certainly much attracted to the handsome and charming Magnus de la Gardie, a nobleman of French and Swedish blood who was long a favorite at her court and whom she married off at last to her cousin Marie Euphrosyne, daughter of Count Palatine. And she certainly flirted, rather in the manner of the great Queen Elizabeth, with suitors whom she had no intention of marrying, particularly with Marie Euphrosyne's brother, Charles Gustavus, whom she ultimately named as her successor. But the idea of marriage and sexual intercourse repelled her. She could not bear to have her body used, as she put it, as a peasant might plow his land. Ironically, when in her later years in Rome she seems to have been more amenable to the idea of sexual intercourse, Cardinal Azzolino, with whom she was much infatuated, failed to respond.

It was different with the melancholy beauty Countess Ebba Sparre, whom the queen called "Belle" and jovially described to diplomats as her "bedfellow." She permitted this favorite to marry the brother of her other, Jacob de la Gardie, who had long pined for Ebba, but insisted that his wife continue to live at court. One of Jacob's intimates wrote exuberantly at the time of the wedding: "Count Jacob is taking the reward from the red mouth of the beautiful Ebba Sparre for all the pain and anguish he has suffered these last three years!"

With an eye to cleaning up the sonnets of Shakespeare, academicians have long insisted that the exchange of extravagant terms of passion between persons of the same sex in the seventeenth century was nothing more than a polite convention. But I am skeptical about this. If you take the words of people literally, even when they purport to be joking, you are just as often right as wrong, and I suspect that Queen Christina may have used the term "bedfellow" with a suggestive wink. Although in her day death by fire could be inflicted on inverts of the lower orders, homosexuality was widely prevalent and even openly accepted in European courts, from that of James I to that of Louis XIV's brother, and it seems naïve to suppose that a female monarch of masculine manners, who maintained an absolute power over her household, even to the extent of once killing a servant, should not have sought the red lips of the favorite whom she called "Belle" in the privacy of their shared chamber.

The second reason usually given for Christina's abdication is her conversion to the Church of Rome. This seems to have sprung from an early detestation of the gloom and priggishness of the Lutheran Church, with its hellfire sermons and intolerance of other sects. Christina noted early in her life that the original split from Rome had generated further splits and that the Protestant churches tended to multiply indefinitely and intolerantly. She had to witness as a girl Oxenstierna's repression of the syncretical movement. In her later years, when she wrote the beginnings of her autobiography, addressing it to the only social superior that she ever acknowledged, God, she had this to say on the subject of her conversion:

> All the respect and admiration that I have had for you all my life, Lord, did not prevent me from being very unbelieving and not at all devout. I did not believe in the religion in which I was brought up. All that they told me did not seem worthy of you. I believed that they made you speak after their fashion, and that they wished to deceive me and made me believe them so that they could govern me, according to their will. I had a mortal hatred for the long and frequent sermons of the Lutherans; but I

knew that I must let them have their way and be
patient, and that I must hide what I thought.
When I was a little older I formed a kind of religion
of my own, awaiting that with which you would
inspire me, for which I had naturally such a strong
inclination. You know how many times, in a language not known to the commonality, I asked for
the grace to be enlightened by you, and I vowed to
obey you even at the price of my life and fortune.

After her abdication in favor of her cousin, who took the
name of Charles X, she went to live in Rome. There were two
important reasons for this step: first, she could expect a gra-
cious reception from the Holy Father of so signal a convert,
and second, where else could she be the only queen? In her
initial splendid years in the eternal city she occupied the
Palazzo Farnese, and it began almost to seem that she might
make her fantasy a reality. People flocked to her court, where
she entertained on a royal scale. She may have anticipated the
dictum of Chateaubriand in a later day: "Whoever has nothing else in life should come and live in Rome."

But trouble was not long in coming. Christina's rude ways
soon offended the cardinals. She felt that she had done
enough for the faith in becoming a Catholic without further
demonstrations of piety, and she made no secret of her delight
in broad jokes, salacious comedies, dirty books and buxom
nudes in paintings by Rubens. And this was all bad enough
when she was rich. Who would put up with it when her
money ran out?

It did not take Christina long to discover that the government of her native land was less than eager to fulfill the heavy
financial commitments exacted by a sovereign who had turned
her back on her inherited duties in order to dissipate the
revenues of her erstwhile subjects in lavish parties for prelates
of a church they abhorred. She learned what King Lear had

learned more painfully on the storm-ridden heath: that if one wishes to retain the prerogatives of majesty, one had better hang on to the powers. As a Catholic she could not hope to regain her former throne, but there was Naples, not far from Rome and groaning, she was told, under the Spanish yoke. Might it not be persuaded to rise against its hated viceroy and fling its gates joyfully open to an Amazonian liberator? Queen of Naples and Sicily would sound quite as well as Queen of Sweden.

One might wish to suppose that Christina had some concern for the liberties of an occupied people, but it seems unlikely. She had been piqued in an etiquette struggle with the Spanish papal ambassador and wanted revenge. In similar fashion, during the negotiations for the Peace of Westphalia, she had tried to carve out an independent principality in Alsace for her favorite, Magnus de la Gardie, using up a Swedish bargaining point for her own personal advantage. And she had not hesitated to urge the sale of Swedish ships and African colonies to make up deficiencies in her pension, or to suggest to the emperor that he come to her aid militarily should Sweden attempt to seize her lands in East Pomerania on the grounds that she was a Catholic. This from the daughter of the empire's archenemy, the fallen victor of Lützen! Christina, like most royalties of her time, never put any country's interest before her own. And so now she turned to Cardinal Mazarin—who, like his predecessor Richelieu, specialized in weakening the opponents of France by promoting civil strife within their borders—to suggest that he help her arrange an insurrection in southern Italy. Should she achieve the crown, it would be only for her lifetime. The Bourbons of France would have the reversion.

Mazarin was quite willing to listen. How delightful to provide Spain with a bloody distraction! Christina went up to Paris to confer with him and was housed, magnificently as usual, in Fontainebleau. But while she was there she discovered that her project had been leaked through the Vatican to the Neapolitan viceroy by Rinaldo Monaldeschi, one of her most trusted officers. Furious, imperious, she summoned the wretched man to her presence, confronted him with the damning evidence, offered him a priest for a final confession and then withdrew from the chamber while he was hacked to death by three clumsy swordsmen.

It was the end of her Neapolitan project and the end of her being taken seriously by the statesmen of Europe. Even had she still been Queen of Sweden she would have had no right to execute a papal subject on French soil. She was at best a lunatic, at worst a murderer. That she spurned Mazarin's project to exonerate her by reporting the episode as a private vendetta between gentlemen of her court suggests the former.

When, some years later, still desperate for funds, she tossed her hat into the ring as a candidate for the vacant throne of Poland, and persuaded the pope to ask his nuncio to broach the proposition to the bishop of Poznan, one of the principal electors, the latter simply treated the idea with derision.

There was nothing more after this for poor Christina *but* derision. When she died in 1689, at sixty-three, in the Palazzo Riario, far less splendid than the Farnese, she was denied her final wish to be buried in the Pantheon amid its memories of classical grandeur. She was, however, the fourth woman to be laid to rest at St. Peter's. But nothing would have really become her but a death like Sophonisbe's, of poison, defeating her vanquishers by a final magnificent gesture. Heroines of the mold of Corneille, it appeared, were still confined to the stage.

XV
The Princesse des Ursins

The princesse des Ursins appropriately ends this survey, for she points directly to the future. She had, as Saint-Simon puts it, an ambition as vast as any man's, and all of a woman's subtlety in implementing it. She studied the male power structure of her time and mastered it, and she came within an inch of accomplishing what no European woman had ever accomplished: making herself a sovereign in her own right. In a day where a self-made man (at least as we use the term) was a rarity, a self-made woman (excluding royal mistresses) was unheard of.

She had another quality that was not characteristic of her era: patriotism. We have learned to regard it as a not unmixed blessing, even at times as a downright curse, but when she became a Spaniard in spirit, it was probably the best thing that could have happened to that beleaguered nation.

She was born in 1642, Anne-Marie de la Trémouille, of an ancient and noble family, daughter of the duc de Noirmoutier, and was married at seventeen to Blaise de Talleyrand, prince de Chalais. She immediately joined the "smart set" of Parisian society, where she became friendly with Madame Scarron, a relationship that was to have momentous consequences more than four decades later. Her French life was

abruptly cut short when she and her husband had to take
refuge in Spain following his participation in one of those
lethal duels in the Place des Vosges, four to a side, that too
outrageously defied the edict of Louis XIV. The young couple
stayed just long enough in Spain for Madame de Chalais to
acquire a basis in the language that was later to be so useful to
her, and then moved to Italy where Chalais died of a sudden
fever. Penniless, childless and alone, but brilliant, beautiful
and charming, his young widow resolved to conquer Rome.

The French colony in the papal see was dominated by the
cardinals de Bouillon and d'Estrées, who soon saw the value to
their government of using this capable woman as a social
center for ecclesiastic and political society. It has been alleged
that Madame de Chalais solidified her position by becoming
the mistress of one or both of these priests, but this did not
prevent them from arranging her marriage to the elderly duc
de Bracciano, a prince of the Orsini family, who was easily
persuaded that he was infatuated with her. As the mistress of
a great palazzo, she now became the queen of Roman society.
Everybody who was anybody went to her receptions.

The poor old husband, naturally enough, soon came to resent being a nonentity in contrast to his spectacular spouse,
and there were money troubles as well. To regulate the questions of her own property in France and to arrange for a
proper pension from the French crown, whose valuable agent
she had now become, the duchess made two extended visits to
Paris, unaccompanied by her probably relieved husband. It
was in the course of these that she met the young duc de
Saint-Simon, whose mother was an old friend of hers, and
utterly fascinated him. His descriptions of her, based on a
much greater personal acquaintance than he enjoyed with
some of his other characters, are perhaps more accurate:

> She was on the tall side and had blue eyes. She said
> whatever she pleased. Her figure was fine; her neck

and shoulders superb; her face, if less than beautiful, charmed. She had an air of nobility, almost of majesty about her, and a natural grace even in the smallest gestures, that I have never seen equaled. She could flatter and cajole with such magical effect that it was impossible to resist her, and yet she always maintained a certain dignity that attracted instead of throwing one off. She spoke wonderfully well of all the great events and personages that she had seen and known.

Saint-Simon also noted that she was a flirt and dressed too youthfully for her age. For all her cleverness and subtlety, she had a nature that was basically direct and frank, at times too much so. She could never do things by halves. People had to be her friends or her enemies. She was passionately loyal to the former and implacable with the latter.

When Bracciano died, his estates were largely seized by creditors, but his widow was able to salvage the palazzo and its contents. The settlement with his family required her to drop her ducal title, and henceforth she styled herself principessa dei Orsini, or princesse des Ursins, as she is known in history. She deliberately alienated her old protector, the Cardinal de Bouillon, by draping the doorway of her palace in violet cloth rather than the black that he had stipulated. This was typical of her. She would jeopardize all of her hard-earned gains rather than submit to even a petty injustice, if she thought she had a decent chance of getting away with it. And she usually did. She counted on her value to the ministers of Louis XIV in spreading propaganda among the Italians, particularly those in the Spanish possessions, in favor of the French candidate to the throne, always about to be vacated, by the ever-dying Carlos II.

The ultimate reward for her services to Versailles came very late in her life, in 1701, when she was almost sixty, an age when most women were either dead or black-garbed widows attending to their impending salvation. Louis XIV, at the cost of a world war, had just placed his grandson, the duc d'Anjou, on the Spanish throne. A marriage had been arranged between the new monarch and the princesse Marie-Louise of Savoy, daughter of Duke Victor Amadeus II and sister of the duchesse de Bourgogne. Who was to escort the young bride from Turin to Madrid and instruct her in her new duties? Who but a loyal French subject, deeply trained in international tensions and intrigues, with the grace and dignity appropriate to the post of camarera-mayor and a fluent knowledge of the three tongues involved? Only such a woman would have a chance of alleviating the xenophobia of the Spaniards while working with the French representatives.

It worked out even better than anticipated. Only one untoward thing happened, from a French viewpoint. Madame des Ursins proved a bit of a Thomas à Becket. She took her new charge too seriously. Her job was to establish a French king with an Italian queen on the Spanish throne. But in doing so, she made them both Spaniards.

It is not difficult to see why the thirteen-year-old Marie-Louise, who had never been out of Savoy and who found herself encased in the rigor of a Spanish court without a single friend, matched to a shy stranger, should have given her heart to this sophisticated, kindly, amusing older woman. "Come, my dear, let us see what we can make out of these odd people and customs!" one can imagine Madame des Ursins beginning. Marie-Louise was fortunate indeed in having a non-Spaniard as her guide. The normal rule in all European nations was that a foreign princess had to be separated from her ladies at the border. Marie-Louise's sister had had to go to Versailles with strangers, though, happily for her, Madame de Maintenon had there been able to play a role similar to that of Madame des Ursins.

Through the queen, Madame des Ursins came also to dominate the king. Philip V was a moody man, well-meaning but inert, whose principal emotional outlet was in an almost frenzied uxoriousness. He was too much of a religious puritan even to consider an extramarital liaison, and his poor little wife had to put up with his extended nightly attentions even when she was sick or pregnant or both. But in return he was docile and easily led. The energy of Madame des Ursins quickly filled the vacuum of his indifference.

To get a sense of the appalling quality of life at the Spanish court that young Marie-Louise had to face, one must read her camarera-mayor on the subject of the ladies who, except for herself, constituted the sole society permitted the queen. They seem to have been the idlest, stupidest creatures imaginable. They did not rise until midday and took siestas in the afternoon. When they were admitted to the presence of the queen,

> After having kneeled to kiss her hand, they took their seats below her and remained dumb. If the queen and I did not talk, there would be no conversation at all. If you ask them if they would like to dance, sing or play an instrument, or even if they want to take a walk or have a game of cards, the answer is invariably no. What can you do with such people? What they can do for themselves, however, is to be continually requesting favors, which, if granted, are accepted smugly as their due.

The men were not much better; all they did was talk about the weather. What did it matter to Marie-Louise that her new friend was almost half a century older than she? At least she was alive. The court was dead.

The war went badly from the start. Philip V had the support of the common people, but the invading forces supporting the Hapsburg candidate were formidable. Madame des Ursins and the royal couple had to work with Spanish bureaucrats, who were paralyzed by red tape, and French government agents who looked upon Spain as a mere auxiliary in a larger conflict. Naturally the camarera-mayor lacked the knowledge and training to handle the massive financial and administrative problems that confronted the government, but having lived in Italy and France, and being mistress of three languages, and having for decades watched the game of power politics at the highest level, she had developed an international point of view and was able accurately to assess the full impact of Iberian insularity. One didn't, as she might have briskly put it, have to be a hen to spot a rotten egg. She could see that Spanish red tape had to be cut if war was to be waged successfully, and she was sophisticated enough to understand that this had to be done with some degree of tact. The great task was to see that capable men were entrusted with the administration. The great danger was that both the Spaniards and French would think she was working for the other. In the end she was bound to slip between these two stools.

There were religious troubles as well. She was appalled by the cruelty of the Inquisition, though she had the sense to realize that it could not be openly opposed. Even with the Gallic church she had had to be careful. Privately, of course, it was different, and her letters have a modern ring. She was disgusted with both Jansenists and anti-Jansenists for letting their differences interfere with the war effort, as she made clear to Madame de Maintenon:

> They should put off their squabbles until we have a peace. Then they can resume them to their heart's content and tear each other's hats off if they please. But right now we have more serious matters to think about. So far as I'm concerned, there is nothing to choose between them, and I always pick a confessor who has neither hate nor enthusiasm for either side.

Complaints that Madame des Ursins did not give sufficient ear to the French representatives poured into Versailles, and Louis XIV began to have grave doubts about his choice of camarera-mayor. A ridiculous episode brought matters to a crisis. The letters to the home office of the French ambassador, the Abbé d'Estrées, were intercepted by order of Philip V and read by Madame des Ursins. Outraged to see in one of these that she was suspected not only of being the mistress of her private secretary, Daubigné, but of actually having married him, she penned indignantly in the margin, "As to marriage, no!" She then wrote a letter of complaint to Torcy, the French minister of foreign affairs, and sent a copy of the offending Estrées' letter to her brother in Paris. Torcy confiscated the brother's copy and showed it to the king.

Louis XIV was incensed, not that his ambassador's letter should be opened (he was used to that) but that a subject of his should dare admit having done so. Madame des Ursins was recalled to France. Queen Marie-Louise was in floods of tears at losing her beloved camarera-mayor. She protested desperately, but Louis was adamant. Madame des Ursins was his subject; Marie-Louise was his granddaughter-in-law. Let them obey.

When Madame des Ursins arrived in Paris, she did so with no hangdog look. Buoyed up by the known favor of the king and queen of Spain, she called upon Madame de Maintenon as an equal and managed to be received by the king. Rarely has a disgrace been so deftly converted to a return to power, and to greater power, too.

She had correctly seen that the key to her problem was Madame de Maintenon. The two women had been friends fifty years before when Madame Scarron had been considerably the social inferior. But there had been a meeting of the minds, a prompt congeniality that both remembered. Each shrewdly assessed the world she faced and admired the other's capacity and determination. Neither was bogged down in the snobbishness or prejudice of the day. It was natural for two such capable, disciplined, attractive persons to lend each other a hand, not only out of a mutual respect but because partnership might prove useful. Madame de Maintenon recognized that Madame des Ursins could extend her influence to Spain. They should continue a dialogue that would be valuable to both governments.

The enemies of Madame de Maintenon, of course, saw in this friendship further evidence of a sinister desire to increase her power. Yet it might have been a simple wish to be of assistance to her monarch. "Madame la princesse des Ursins will shortly be returning to Spain," she wrote. "I must take care of her and do all I can to overcome the coldness of the duchesse de Bourgogne and the dryness of the king."

She succeeded. Louis XIV spent hours at Marly closeted with his wife and the princess, and learned to relish the latter's wit and conversation. Both women had the social discipline of an earlier time; their manners pleased a monarch who was becoming disgusted with the laxity of the young. The princess had the same mixture of charm and forcefulness that had pleased him in his spouse.

Did Madame des Ursins really want to go back to Spain? The court at Madrid must have looked arid and stiff from the halls and gardens of Versailles. But Louis XIV and Madame de Maintenon were now prepared to make things easier for her. She would have as French ambassador not one of those lofty, narrow-minded, quarrelsome priests but an able bourgeois, Amelot—realistic, hardheaded and not consumed in idle questions of precedence. Furthermore, Amelot would be instructed to defer in every decision to the camarera-mayor. The latter's allowance would also be substantially increased. One of her brothers would be made a duke; the other was promised a cardinal's hat. When Louis XIV came around, he did not do things by halves.

The princess duly returned to Spain, and with renewed

authority, but she soon found that she had need of every bit of it. The Anglo-Portuguese forces had occupied Madrid, and Philip V was obliged to flee to Burgos. She relates her plight with good spirit to Madame de Maintenon:

> Let me amuse you by describing my quarters. They consist of one tiny room, that seems only twelve by twelve. One side consists of a window that won't shut. A low door opens into the queen's chamber; another, to a crooked passageway, so badly paved that you risk breaking your neck even when it's lit. My walls may be white; it's hard to tell, they're so dirty. The sole furniture consists of my traveling bed, a folding chair and a wood table that serves for desk, bureau and buffet. I have no kitchen and no money to keep one. But the queen and I manage to laugh about it all.

Although she had at one time been sufficiently discouraged with the war to envisage the loss of Spain and the possible retirement of Philip V to his Italian dominions, she now seemed to draw heart from adversity. Never again after Burgos did she admit so much as the possibility of defeat. Her heart beat like a Spaniard's. She saw that the nation was not to be judged by a handful of grandees who changed sides whenever it looked as if the enemy might prevail. She had seen something of the people, and had measured the hardships they were willing to endure for a monarch whom they deemed their own under God. Philip V to them was no longer a French prince. He had been named by Carlos II, and he was adopted by his new nation. They would fight on grimly until the English and Germans and Portuguese had been expelled. "How could Louis XIV abandon his grandson now?" Madame des Ursins demanded. Yet there was every evidence that he was considering it. The war was going disastrously in the Lowlands; the French were looking about to cut their losses.

Madrid, however, was at last retaken and Philip V prepared
a triumphal return. The royal party stopped en route at the
Escorial, which the princess now saw with Iberian eyes:

> It is magnificent, very grand indeed, with admirable
> paintings and works of marble and bronze. The
> chapel is fine, though St. Peter's in Rome does spoil
> one's eye for other churches. And the pantheon,
> where all the kings since Charles V are encrypted,
> inspires both fear and awe.

Reinforced by the popular demonstrations over the returning sovereign, the camarera-mayor summarily dismissed
those of the queen's ladies who had not followed her to Burgos. The court could not be made more efficient, but it might
be made more loyal. The emergency was still critical. Word
was received that the dismemberment of Spain might be one
of the conditions of the approaching peace talks. Madame de
Maintenon, who had divined the intensification of her
friend's pro-Spanish feelings, wrote her: "You are to be pitied,
Madame, as at once a good French woman and a good Spaniard."

Yet when, at the end of 1707, Madame des Ursins held up
for baptism the infant prince of the Asturias, heir to the ancient crown of Charles V and of Philip II, and a great-grand-
son of her own master, Louis XIV, when she saw that her
mission, as originally conferred upon her by the French, could
still be completed successfully if people would only fight on,
she must have felt justified in ignoring the later amendments
to that mission by persons in faraway Versailles who had no
true concept of or concern with the destiny of Spain. She had
been sent, as she saw it anyway, to establish Philip on his
throne and to ensure the continuance of Spain as a nation
under his rule. Well, then, she would do it!

Her correspondence with Madame de Maintenon now became increasingly acrimonious, but they never came to a

break. Madame des Ursins would not give Louis XIV grounds
for a charge of treason to the French cause. She always insisted that she was his loyal subject, but that in Spain she
must operate as she felt she had to operate—until such time
as he saw fit to order her return to France. That command
was never forthcoming. Louis in 1709 was obliged to break off
his peace talks that he had initiated because the enemy terms
were too stiff. So long as he was obliged to continue the war
and continue to back Spain, he was far better off with the
princesse des Ursins in Madrid.

But when the terrible war went badly again, Louis went
back again to considering ways of abandoning his grandson.
Madame des Ursins grew more and more political in her correspondence with Madame de Maintenon, outlining, in what
amounted in one case almost to a brief, the methods of raising
money and supplies. At this point Madame de Maintenon
began to retreat. She even suggested that her friend, having
written of military matters in such detail, must have expected
her letter to be passed on to higher authority, and she reminded her that at Versailles "we don't like women to concern themselves with state business." If Saint-Simon could
have seen that! Yet there was truth in it. Madame de Maintenon's position in Versailles was far less powerful than that of
the princess in Madrid. The former could not even persuade
Louis XIV to permit Madame des Ursins' nephew to accept a
grandeeship from Philip V.

Madame des Ursins survived as camarera-mayor until the
treaty of Utrecht, supreme in Madrid and at least tolerated in
Versailles, but she played a less noble role in making the peace
than she had in carrying on the war. She threw all of her
energies and resources into carving out of the international
settlements a small principality for herself. There were plenty
of these at the disposition of the Holy Roman Emperor; it was
only a question of bringing the right pressure to bear. The
princess worked for herself now as avidly as she had ever

worked for Spain, and one can hardly escape the feeling that she would have been willing to jeopardize the national gains to obtain her personal ones. She must have felt that she was owed something, and she knew that if she didn't take care of herself, nobody else would.

Why did she care so? Because in her day precedence and rank were hard realities; a "majesty," even of a state as big as a minute, was entitled to sit in an armchair in the presence of Louis XIV himself; he had no superior on the globe, and if, armed with such a privilege, he was also possessed of the brain and fortune of a Madame des Ursins, he was as impregnable as a mortal could be. But what was the powerful camarera-mayor arming herself against? Everything. Louis XIV held a grudge against her because of her independence in Madrid; his nephew, the duc d'Orléans, the probable future regent of France, was her mortal enemy because of their quarrels when he had been a general in Spain; the pope resented her failure to heal differences between Madrid and the papal see, and Philip V—well, who could count on a Bourbon? Lovely Marie-Louise might be devoted to her, but lovely Marie-Louise was gravely, perhaps fatally ill.

The principality fell through, and the poor young queen did die, in 1714. In view of the drastic sexual needs of Philip V and of his curious puritanism, it was essential to get him a new mate at the earliest possible moment. Alberoni, a wily Italian priest who had attached himself firmly to the Spanish court, persuaded Madame des Ursins that the perfect candidate would be Elizabeth Farnese, daughter of the duke of Parma—hardly a dazzling match for the Catholic king but one that might provide a grateful queen to the camarera-mayor and an easy one to dominate. Actually, Alberoni had already laid his plans to prepare the new queen, who had an assertive and imperious disposition, to run the princesse des Ursins out of the kingdom on the very day that she was presented to her supposed new mistress.

The famous scene occurred at Jadraque, near the border, when the princesse des Ursins, in full court regalia, went to meet the bride of Philip V. The two women were alone together for a short while; we do not know what was said. But suddenly Elizabeth Farnese screamed for her guard and ordered that "this madwoman" be driven posthaste into France. The unhappy camarera-mayor was clapped into a carriage without even a cloak and driven to the border in weather so freezing that one of the coachmen lost a hand. She was never to return to Spain. Philip V, at first distressed when he heard of her rough treatment, was quickly taken into the arms of his determined new spouse, and after that night he never wasted another thought on the person who had been his intimate friend and favorite for thirteen years.

Louis XIV died the following year. There was nobody now at Versailles who could do anything for her. But the indomitable old woman made her way back to Italy and set herself up in a Roman palazzo where she survived until 1722, a legend to those of the younger generations who knew enough history to be attracted to her gatherings. Among these was the English pretender, James III. Madame des Ursins had become a leader of his little circle by the time of his death. Who knows? She might have been dreaming of repeating in London the great role she had played in Madrid.

With her the splendid age lost its last survivor. The eighteenth century would boast many famous women, and there would be at least two, the empress Maria Theresa and Catherine the Great, who would demonstrate the courage and executive flair of Madame des Ursins, but as suggested in the beginning of this survey, it was to be in too many ways the age of the Pompadour and du Barry, the age of charm, of interior decoration, of Boucher, of Fragonard, the era of a feminism that was almost effeminate. Of course, I am dealing in generalities—what else is history?—but I do not sense in the eighteenth century the same fiber of female self-assertion that

Louis XIV, that ultimate male chauvinist, strove so hard to put down. It took all the gravity of the nineteenth century to make up for the frivolity of its predecessor, so that in the twentieth century women would be able to pick up where those of the seventeenth had left off. The vision of Corneille has become almost contemporary; the false dawn, a true one.

In Lieu of a Bibliography

I do not see the value of citing the sources of secondary works consulted or in listing such standard sources as the memoirs of the duc de Saint-Simon, the letters of Madame de Sévigné or the essays of Sainte-Beuve, but I should like to recommend to those interested in my subject the following works that I found particularly illuminating:

La Princesse des Ursins, by Marianne Cermakian, Didier, Paris, 1969

Madame de Maintenon, by Mme. Saint-René Taillandier, Hachette, Paris, 1920

The Backstairs Dragon, a life of Robert Harley, by Elizabeth Hamilton, Hamish Hamilton, London, 1969

Daughter of France, by V. Sackville-West, Doubleday, Garden City, N.Y., 1959

The Great Duchess, by Iris Butler, Funk & Wagnalls, New York, 1968

William and Mary, by Henri and Barbara Van der Zee, Alfred A. Knopf, New York, 1972

Queen Anne, by Edward Gregg, Routledge & Kegan Paul, London, 1980

The Sun King, by Nancy Mitford, Harper & Row, New York, 1966

Index